INTERNATIONAL MERGER

by Foreign Entanglements

by Arthur R. Thompson, *CEO*

THE JOHN BIRCH SOCIETY
Appleton, Wisconsin

Cover designed by Katie Carder

First Printing
Copyright © 2014 by The John Birch Society

Published by
THE JOHN BIRCH SOCIETY
770 N. Westhill Boulevard
Appleton, Wisconsin 54914
www.jbs.org

LC Control Number
2013957836
Printed in the United States of America
ISBN: 1-881919-12-9

"The great rule of conduct for us in regard to foreign nations is in extending our commercial relations, to have with them as little political connection as possible.... It is our true policy to steer clear of permanent alliances with any portion of the foreign world.'

— George Washington,
Farewell Address, 1796

Contents

Introduction

The people of the United States are being fed a constant diet of treaties, agreements, pacts, and partnerships, and most of them are sold under the banner of free trade. Never in our nation's 230-year history has our country negotiated and entered into as many as we have seen over the past couple of decades. It's time to take a closer look at what is involved in these agreements, regardless of their stated purpose, to see if there is a recurring pattern.

When dealing with the issue of foreign policy where treaties and trade agreements are created, two principles must be kept in mind, and they both have to do with the freedom and independence of the American people.

First, is the oft-repeated adage coined by the English nobleman known as Lord Acton:

Power tends to corrupt, and absolute power corrupts absolutely.

Since the power he referred to resides in government, an added rule is that the larger the government and the more power it has, having taken it away from the people, the more corrupt that government is likely to be.

Second, other warnings given by the men who founded our great American experiment in liberty had some very sage advice for us concerning foreign policy:

> It is our true policy to steer clear of permanent alliances with any portion of the foreign world....
>
> — George Washington, 1796

> Commerce with all nations, alliance with none, should be our motto.
>
> — Thomas Jefferson, 1799

> I deem [one of] the essential principles of our government [to be] peace, commerce, and honest friendship with all nations, entangling alliances with none....
>
> — Thomas Jefferson, 1801

Here we have two lessons that have a direct bearing on the modern pacts, such as the free trade agreements that our government is negotiating and signing with countries around the globe. There always is a desire for commerce, but there is great danger in forming alliances that really have very little to do with trade and have a lot to do with the accumulation of power, particularly international power through regional institutions, such as the European Union, and worldwide institutions, such as the United Nations.

The titles given these various treaties and agreements may suggest benefits for the participants and their peoples, but their texts contain precisely what Lord Acton and America's founders warned about.

Let us quote one more American, Mark Twain:

> The only difference between reality and fiction is that fiction needs to be credible.

What we will be discussing will at times seem to be incredible because it is real, a reality rarely discussed when discussing U.S. foreign policy. However, it is a reality that anyone can verify online if there is a desire to do so. We will supply references from time to time so that this valuable tool can be put to use.

1
Under the Banner of Commerce, Our Nation Is Forming Permanent Alliances

In various pacts the U. S. government has entered into since the end of World War II, we have been witnessing entanglements that deliver power to international organizations through regional institutions, such as NAFTA (the North American Free Trade Agreement), and worldwide institutions, such as the United Nations. This is the consistent pattern that runs throughout all of our foreign dealings.

The titles on these pacts promote an idea that is very different from the actual contents of the packages, although there are hints of their contents from time to time even within the titles. And, all too often, negotiations are kept secret not only from the American people but from Congress as well. Repeatedly, elected officials see the agreements only a short time before they are asked to vote on them. Sometimes, they never see the documents. Rarely do they have enough time to thoroughly read and understand them.

Lack of Transparency

Over the last two or three decades, increasing reliance on secrecy has come to dominate the federal administration and the congressional *leadership*. This can be readily seen in proposed groundbreaking laws and treaties. Once enacted, secrecy remains a presence in the implementation of the various pacts.

In addition to secrecy, there exists a tactic that has been used on occasion to gain approval of controversial treaties. It involves moves by the Senate leadership, based on the ratification provision of Article II, Section 2 — "provided two thirds of the Senators *present* concur" (emphasis added), that the majority of the Senate would reject. We will give an example in Chapter Nine

Let us state up front that we believe that a large majority of Americans would support genuine free trade between the businessmen of one country and those of another. But, the results of trade pacts are something far different from the promises given to the American people and Congress as reasons to support the agreements.

If trade between countries were truly free, there would be no need for hundreds or thousands of pages to spell out what it shall or shall not entail.

Ask yourself if the following is the kind of agreement

you could support: A single piece of paper signed by leaders of two or more countries stating that there will be no interference by the respective governments with the transactions between their businessmen. Except for cases where fraud or national security considerations exist, the government will have nothing to offer. It's all very simple.

Some individuals will claim that the trade issue is so complex and so important that there is a need to spell out every minute detail. This is a smokescreen designed to discourage anyone from questioning what the mountains of paper say and mean. The agreement should not be complex and neither should the powers of a properly created government.

Keep in mind that our nation's Constitution as the "supreme law of the land" governs the entire "complex" United States by spelling out what the federal government may do. *And it was originally written on four sheets of paper!*

Why then do negotiations for free trade agreements take years to complete? Studies made about these negotiations even take a great deal of time and money. And finally, why are the finalized agreements as thick as municipal telephone books?

Ask yourself some further questions: Have trade agreements negotiated in the past few decades actually added to America's economic vitality? How many jobs and factories moved out of our country as a result of these pacts? Have any of these agreements benefited small and medium-sized businesses, the heart of the American economy? Or, have they mainly helped the multinational corporations whose leaders boast of their international loyalties and their lack of concern about the value of our nation's independence?

If the answers to these questions are negative regarding our economy, then why do we continue to seek a remedy that has proven to fail? Is there a different motivation behind so-called free trade agreements?

One of the reasons these negotiations take so long is that the people who represent the multinationals need a pact that helps them win in a competitive market. In short, they don't want a level playing field. They have the ears of the leaders of various countries who also like the idea of government involvement and interference. In addition, they have an army of highly paid lobbyists who are in constant contact with negotiators and others connected with the process.

These corporations and organizations are sometimes referred to as "stakeholders," since they have a "stake" in seeing the agreements go forward and having a seat at the negotiating table. It is not unusual for the negotiating parties to hold gala affairs to bring the stakeholders into the picture while wining and dining them. If there should be any doubts by stakeholders as to the motivation of the negotiators behind a new pact, they are assuaged in the limelight of the pageantry. After all, so many "important people" can't be wrong.

The stakeholders range from the obvious left-oriented organizations to the not so obvious internationalists. In the case of the Transatlantic Trade and Investment Partnership (TTIP), for which negotiations between the United States and the European Union began on July 8, 2013, stakeholders range from the Sierra Club, Friends of the Earth, and AFL-CIO, to the National Chamber of Commerce and National Manufacturing Association. The latter two have moved miles away from their early years of promoting American business and are now promoting international business initiatives. The negotiators may differ on nuances, but not with the idea of merging economic structures.

Lobbying for a better "deal" is the most innocent of the reasons why negotiations drag on and result in convoluted language that only a lawyer steeped in legalistic bureaucratese can decipher. Other reasons have the motivation that reminded us of the aforementioned quip by Mark Twain.

Some of the more recent proposals have titles that use the seemingly innocuous word "Partnership." These include the Security and Prosperity Partnership (SPP) of 2005, the Trans-Pacific Partnership (TPP) scheduled for completion by 2014, the proposed Transatlantic Trade and Investment Partnership (TTIP) scheduled for completion by 2015, and more. What does "partnership" among nations have to do with free businessmen of one nation trading with the free businessmen from another country? The answer: Articles written about the plans to create these agreements refer to the need for international rules and cooperation.

Rules are not free trade. Rules are control by government of business, labor, and investment. That's the entire sphere of commerce. Careful reading of these pacts shows them to be full of such language.

Even those who advocate creation of the pacts or are involved in the negotiations refer to controls and regulations. For instance, in a recent article authored by TTIP drumbeater Tyson Marker in the Council on Foreign Relations (CFR) journal *Foreign Affairs*, there is a description of the aim of the Transatlantic Trade and Investment Partnership:

In the broadest terms, a U.S.-EU trade deal

would allow the United States and Europe to maintain their sway over *global economic governance*. Both recognize that their ability *to set global rules* will diminish as economic power shifts to the Asia-Pacific region. In the coming decade, no one power will be able to drive the *international agenda*. But if they join forces, the United States and Europe can channel their combined economic weight *to keep control of the reins of the global economic order*. [Emphasis added.]

Global economic governance? Global rules? International agenda? Global economic order? Marker has made our point!

Karel De Gucht, European Commissioner for Trade for the European Commission, wrote a paper issued by the Committee on International Trade of the European Parliament on February 21, 2013. In it he stated:

A future deal between the world's two most important economic powers will be a game-changer. Together, we will form the largest free trade zone in the world. This deal will set the standard — not only for our future bilateral trade and investment but also for *the development of global rules.* [Emphasis added.]

We could quote others who are moving these plans forward and have issued similar statements. The emphasized portions in the above statements demonstrate that this is not really free trade regardless of the labels applied. They show that there are surely going to be international regulations and controls rather than free enterprise-based trade.

These pacts also call for the establishment of international arbiters, courts, and other mechanisms whose powers can and will supersede the court system of the United States and subject our economic life to international control.

North American Free Trade Agreement (NAFTA)

The 1994 North American Free Trade Agreement involving the United States, Mexico, and Canada certainly makes our case. Commonly referred to as NAFTA, it resulted in the establishment of multilateral panels and tribunals. Chapter 11 of NAFTA, for instance, created a tribunal possessing authority to rule on trade disputes between citizens of any of the three nations. Other chapters in the NAFTA agreement outline further judicial remedies to settle disputes.

Very few people have ever heard of this NAFTA court. And there is no process to appeal its decisions by American citizens in an American court. Further, investors who allege that a host government has breached its obligations under NAFTA's Chapter 11 may have recourse to either of two arbitral mechanisms: the UN-related World Bank's International Center for the Settlement of Investment Disputes or the rules established by the UN Commission for International Trade Law.[1]

When seeking justice, the American businessman must appeal to NAFTA tribunals or to one or both of the UN entities named above. Beyond the time and expense involved in an extremely complicated process, the chances of gaining a favorable ruling are slim.

The fact that a NAFTA court would even exist was well-hidden within the pact. It appears that very few people outside of those who wrote the agreement even knew about it until after it had been ratified. Certainly the congressmen and senators who approved it didn't.

Former U.S. Congressman Abner Mikva, who became a NAFTA judge after years of representing a Chicago-area district, stated of the tribunal, "If Congress

---

1. For a complete look at international courts and tribunals, go to the website of the Project on International Courts and Tribunals (http://www.pict-pcti.org/). You will likely be amazed at the complexity of the controls that already exist to deal with Americans and others.

had known there was anything like this in NAFTA, they would never have voted for it." NAFTA's text fills 2,000 pages but its title includes the word "free." It received influential backing from David Rockefeller and Henry Kissinger, two acknowledged internationalists who described the agreement as an important step toward creation of, in their words, a "new world order."

How much time, effort, and money do you think it would cost an American businessman to appeal a case before an international court? And what do you think his chances for success would be if he did appeal?

The worst aspect of this is that our system is based on reliance on our own Supreme Court that is supposed to serve as the final judicial arbiter as well as a check on the power of the federal government. According to the Constitution, power to regulate commerce with foreign nations rests with Congress. But international courts erase this portion of our system and become the final arbiters. Thus, the constitutional mandate for regulation of commerce by Congress is lost to international organizations, whose judges use a growing set of rules being formed by the United Nations and other international institutions, not our Congress or the American people.[2]

2. See the *New York Times* article "Review of U.S. Rulings by NAFTA Tribunals Stirs Worries," April 18, 2004.

This system is a direct attack on the checks and balances that we have within our system of government among the legislative, executive, and judicial branches. It takes the Supreme Court out of the equation and places its responsibility with an international court.

The checks and balances of our government are in serious jeopardy if jurisdiction and court opinions are relegated to foreign courts and bodies. Supreme Court Justice Sandra Day O'Connor, on October 28, 2003, stated that:

> I suspect that over time we will rely increasingly
> ... on international and foreign courts in *examining domestic issues*. [Emphasis added.]

Not just international arbitration, but in deciding domestic issues!

This NAFTA tribunal is an example of similar creations in other United Nations or UN-related pacts. When you start to research all of this, you immediately find yourself entangled in a huge web of treaties needing cross-referencing, etc. It is very difficult to figure out what's going on in this maze of verbiage. It is a lesson on what foreign *entanglements* really mean.

Since the approval of NAFTA by Congress in 1993, the integration of the three economies of North America has proceeded at a sharp pace. While for some this may seem to be something to be happy about, the downside is that economic integration has always been followed by political integration. (See Chapter Four – The European Union.)

World Economic Stability

In the name of providing world economic and trade stability, the World Trade Organization (WTO) was established. Which brings up another question: If the WTO were intended to bring about trade stability and fair trade around the world, why is it necessary to duplicate its efforts with myriad pacts dealing with the same issue?

After all, these pacts are entered into by nations who are already members of the WTO. Members of WTO agreed to grant Most Favored Nation (MFN) status to each other. Renamed "permanent normal trade relations," the former MFN status should be sufficient for trade. The big difference between membership in the WTO and participation in these free trade pacts is the formulation of extra-governmental obligations for the so-called free trade agreements.

In addition to immersing our nation in NAFTA, U.S. leaders and leaders of numerous other nations have submitted to the WTO. How this international trade group came into existence is revealing. In 1948, the United Nations created the International Trade Organization, whose main architect was American State Department official Alger Hiss. Hiss eventually went to prison for lying about his espionage activities on behalf of the Soviet Union, and thus was exposed as an agent of Russia's spy apparatus under Stalin.

Later, the International Trade Organization was renamed the World Trade Organization, which is currently listed by the UN as one of its "related" organizations. Congress approved U.S. membership in the WTO in 1994. Just prior to being named Speaker of the House of Representatives in 1995, Congressman Newt Gingrich (R-Ga.) sought the immersion of our government into the WTO even though he warned about its power during his testimony before the House Ways and Means Committee in June 1994. He told his colleagues, "I am just saying that we need to be honest about the fact that we are transferring from the United States at a practical level significant authority to a new organization. This is a transformational moment." In a lame-duck session of Congress later that year, he then voted for what he had warned others about.

Like NAFTA, the WTO has its own judicial body whose decisions are final unless rejected by unanimous agreement of all 159 WTO member nations. This makes it impossible to overturn any decision. The WTO has ruled against the U.S. in matters involving tax laws, cotton subsidies, steel tariffs, and more. The threat of a boycott aimed at America by foreign trade groups such as the European Union has been cited by several administrations as the reason why the U.S. must continue to submit to WTO rulings. It is a Catch-22.

2
Partnership

Partnership is a word much in need of close examination and understanding. Partnerships between two, or several, countries involve contracts that limit the ability of a person, business and/or country to act on its own. In other words, once their nation forms a partnership, the citizens of a free country are prevented from making independent decisions and are confined to the rules, regulations, and decisions of a majority within that partnership, whatever they may be. Is this free trade?

A real and uncomplicated partnership is a business transaction between citizens, not nations. In these newer-style trade partnerships formed among nations, however, governments make the rules, not the people involved in the producing and trading of goods.

In the new type of partnership, governments decide the rules and regulations while independent businesses and workers are forced to obey. This can cause a delay in arriving at decisions or the handing down of detrimental decisions favoring foreign businesses or foreign labor groups. In other words, free enterprise and competition are stifled because they are now under the purview of factors and commissions outside of the United States.

Since these partnerships are between nations (or groupings such as the European Union) and not businesses, the rules actually covering transactions will be made by forces other than those who produced the products or wish to purchase them. Therefore, whoever has the most influence within the group of nations will receive the best "deal."

Ask yourself another question: Does doing business overseas sometimes necessitate looking the other way when dealing with the leaders of a corrupt system who have their hands out for bribes or "incentives" before they agree to do business? The answer is obvious. Some nations are notorious for not doing business until "the palm is greased." In many countries, the problem is endemic and systemic — part of their culture — and no government agreement will change that.

In some countries, the rulers themselves expect to be bribed before they allow a business to operate in their country. Over the years, the media have reported many such examples. In some instances, funds to pay the bribe came from tax money taken from American citizens. It seems that the only time this is reported, however, is when a ruler falls out of favor with the internationalists. Realistically, can anyone compete fairly within a system that ties one's hands even before buying or selling goods starts? This type of corruption or statism is widely practiced.

In any case, working with an international or corrupt system places an honest American businessman at a real disadvantage. Think of how this will apply once any trade agreement between a free country, such as the U.S., and a corrupt state or grouping of states, such as the EU, takes over. How much would Americans have to bend in order to make a "trade" deal?

What is a partnership? It is a contract creating the condition of association with a common purpose and with a formal structure. In a word: merger.

3
Fair Trade

Too many believe that free trade is fair trade. Fair trade is impossible between two unequal economic systems or two unequal political systems. The two or more systems must be brought into harmony for the trade to be on the proverbial "level playing field." This is the hidden agenda within the type of trade agreements being negotiated today: bringing our system more in harmony with the rest of the world. But the rest of the world doesn't have the freedoms protected by the U.S. Constitution.

There have been many studies of how fair trade can be achieved. One was provided by Dr. Lewis E. Lloyd. In his youth, Dr. Lloyd was an eager supporter of free trade. Later, as an official of Michigan's Dow Chemical Company, he studied its pros and cons and ended up completely reversing his earlier belief. His 1955 book *Tariffs: The Case for Protectionism* dwells in part on a listing of eight conditions he insisted must be met if nation-to-nation trade were truly free and fair. Without supplying his ample commentary about each, the conditions he headlined are:

1. Taxes must be comparable.
2. A single monetary system must be in use.
3. There must be uniform business laws.
4. Similar business ethics must prevail.
5. There must be uniform wage rates.
6. Maximum labor mobility must exist across borders.
7. There must be freedom from the threat of war.
8. All of the above would have to be enforced by a world government.

Dr. Lloyd concluded that there would have to be a "world government" if there were to be truly "free" trade. He didn't want that any more than this writer does.

When his book was published in 1955, Dr. Lloyd readily admitted that the conditions needed for worldwide free trade had not been met and, as long as the special interests, customs, and practices in each of the world's nations hadn't been overcome, they could not be met. But he noted that all eight of these conditions existed on a smaller scale within the (then) 48 states of our country. (State taxes varied but the national taxes were universal.) In our country, there was even a national Constitution akin to the world government he

19

claimed would be necessary for worldwide free trade. It governed the states along with a voluntary acceptance of the other conditions.

But the system in America was unique and a world government would not be able to duplicate it. A world constitution over the many sovereign and varied nations would be, of course, impossible without creating an all-powerful world government. Moreover, there would be no freedom remaining under such an all-powerful world government. Which is why Karl Marx endorsed free trade: to use it to help install world government. More on this later in this chapter.

Partnerships between nations rather than between businessmen constitute foreign entanglements and are surely not "free trade." A partnership between nations is not free enterprise. It is a merger of at least some aspects of each nation's economic life. It requires what Dr. Lloyd pointed to. Some agreements go even further and start to form new layers of international government that draw in other nations. This is what happened to once-independent European nations with the development of the European Union.

The results of all free trade agreements have been the opposite of their promised benefits. Yet the benefits that can't be delivered have been sold to Americans to get them to agree to the pacts. These agreements have built up foreign economies to the detriment of the American businessman and worker. This has been especially true of NAFTA.

Problems with NAFTA were pointed out in warnings issued by such organizations as The John Birch Society and such personages as former presidential candidate H. Ross Perot. His predictions of business leaving America for Mexico, and then China, have occurred and harmed our economy. Perot referred to the "giant sucking sound" that would be created by business being drawn elsewhere. What he feared has happened.

Since NAFTA was adopted nearly 20 years ago, the gradual decline of American industry has been spread out over a decade and a half. Nearly an entire generation of voters has never experienced the American economy without NAFTA. What they see is what they believe has always been the American condition.

Similarly, older generations experienced the gradual changes wrought by NAFTA over ensuing years. They got used to what was occurring and the memory of years past faded. Did we used to live in a golden age? No, but conditions were better economically. We now live with a less-than-robust industrial base because it has been severely weakened.

Now that this has become a problem, solutions are being offered to us by the same people who created NAFTA. These are a super NAFTA involving Europe (TTIP) and a proposed duplicate in the Pacific (TPP).

Who Benefits From These Agreements?

First, it is the international corporations and international banks. These institutions are flourishing under the free trade agreements. But the average businessman and worker who produce goods in America haven't benefited. Business is down while unemployment is up and the real statistics about people looking for work are hidden deep within government reports. Many of the dire ramifications of unemployment are not felt directly *due to an array of government benefits being provided.*

The "unemployed" are counted only if they are collecting, or trying to collect, unemployment compensation. Those who are not counted include many whose unemployment funds have run out, and those working part time because they can't find any other work. A part-time worker isn't counted as unemployed, yet you can say that they are half-unemployed. (Part-time employees now make up nearly ten percent of our population.) The true numbers of unemployed are double what the government statistics state. The unemployment figures in the countries in the European Union are much higher. They may contain a clue of what the true figures should be here.

Unemployment in the EU ranges to as high as 27 percent. And, in many EU countries unemployment has continued to rise. Welfare is being supplied to many, but this can't go on forever.

In the United States, one in seven is receiving food stamps. The numbers of people on welfare are down because the federal government has transferred recipients to the Social Security disability program — which has ballooned. These people are still on the government dole, but they are no longer listed as "welfare" recipients (or unemployed). The two combined lists continue to grow at an alarming rate. By manipulating the process and the figures it produces, government gives a false picture that has us believing that victory in the War on Poverty has been won. Actual figures expose the lie. It's another government-run no-win war.

For those who are fortunate enough to be working, wages are off from the 1980s level in real purchasing power due to inflation. We are told that inflation should be measured by a rise in prices. This is only the manifestation of inflation. In actuality, a good older dictionary will tell you that inflation is an increase in the money supply. The net effect is the rise in prices because the newly created dollars (mostly the work of the Federal Reserve) derive their value by stealing the value of existing dollars — including yours and mine. What is inflated is the number of dollars put into circulation!

What cost X amount a few years ago, now costs X times the ratio of the more dollars in circulation today. This is a hidden form of taxation that covers deficits and a string of unconstitutional programs such as foreign aid and unconstitutional federal agencies. Yet very few Americans can explain the phenomenon, which is caused by government and government-created agencies. They wrongly blame the supermarket owner or the gasoline supplier.

The stock market may be reaching new highs, but these are not true highs when you factor in inflation. If this is done, the recent record Dow-Jones figures are actually off 25 percent over previous highs. And, this is according to the official inflation rates, which aren't reliable. There are some who claim that inflation is much higher than what the government says it is. Ask whoever shops regularly for the family's needs if the price of basic commodities hasn't risen more than the published official rate of inflation.

What has been done was started with a muddled

redefinition of inflation and continued with increasing reliance on figures that don't tell the honest truth.

Why bring this all up? Simply to illustrate that our economy is not as rosy as our government's press releases state, and that trade agreements have not helped the situation.

What *is* flourishing is the growth of government both at home and abroad. The burden of NAFTA trade courts is only one contributor to this growth. The formation of commissions, committees, boards — entirely new bureaucracies built every time a new accord is signed — contributes to more growth of the participating governments.

This increase in government power is happening to the detriment of the freedom of the average individual. Some of this growth results from the imposition of international controls and regulations required in agreements already made, and from our membership in various United Nations entities. Many of these new regulations are being imposed without a vote of the people or Congress. Once Congress enacts U.S. participation in a new agreement, the regulations flow out of the necessarily expanded international bureaucracy and Congress allows itself to be pushed aside.

Second, government benefits from these new agreements. Many regulations and controls that wouldn't ordinarily be passed by Congress get through and become compulsory when they are attached to or in connection with international agreements. This happens often because the pacts are presented as if the United Nations requires such action under some other agreement.

Much of this is being done in the name of security and prosperity, or the oft-cited claim of free trade, all of which everyone wants — except those who have studied the pacts. Again, packaging gimmicks are designed to gain the support of the American people and, through them, approval by Congress. After all, who could possibly be against security and prosperity? No one — unless he or she recognizes that these are false labels on agreements that will lead to more government and less freedom for the people.

Ask yourself some other questions: What government agency created since 1933 has solved the problem which it was supposedly created to solve? How many government agencies went "out of business" because they failed or were successfully targeted by an aroused public? (A few were canceled but later restarted with a new name and new management by a different government bureau.) Were any abolished because they had solved the problem pointed to as the reason for being created in the first place? Government does not do a very good job of solving problems.

In fact, it can arguably be stated that the multiplicity of agencies has made matters worse. Campaigns against poverty, drugs, energy imports, etc., come to mind. How can anyone believe that decisions arrived at by current leaders in government will solve so-called trade issues when similar decisions reached by previous administrations didn't accomplish any positive results? The evidence shows that all they have done is to make various problems worse.

Put yourself in the position of a government bureaucrat. The size of the agency and number of employees depend on the perceived problem you were formed to solve. If you solve the problem, you and hundreds, perhaps thousands of government employees would be out of work. If the problem gets worse, it would mean more employees and a higher management position for you. What decision would you make? Solve the problem or find a reason to grow your department?

Government has a consistent habit of using economic downturns and any other crisis to expand its size and scope. The federal government enters into trade agreements that hurt our economy, and then its leaders point to increasing numbers of people who need assistance because of the bad economy as an excuse to enter into even more free trade agreements.

The bursting of the so-called housing bubble didn't cause all of the economic downturn starting in 2008. Recovery would have been accomplished in a short period of time if our nation would have had a strong industrial base, and government simply got out of the way. The base that led to the creation of wealth has been eroded by a combination of wealth going overseas, the steady maniacal purchasing of imported goods, bailouts to foreign banks and countries engineered by the Federal Reserve, conglomerates forcing small business-es out of competition, and industry moving anywhere but in the United States. Most of the economic turndown can't be attributed to the housing bubble. Much of it was caused by free trade agreements.

Recovery was actually hurt by government pouring money into favorite industries and select pork barrel proj-ects rather than allowing the market to drive recovery.

Consider this argument: Can anyone honestly argue that our government is not moving more and more toward socialism? If a government is moving the people toward socialism domestically, will that government have any less of a similar goal in the foreign policy arena? Since it is the same people who drive both domestic and foreign policy, the answer seems obvious.

Perhaps it is time to look to see if the desires of our own government leaders are the same as those of the American people. The problems we are alluding to persist within both political parties and cannot be blamed on a single party.

Remember the words of Lord Acton: "Power tends to corrupt, and absolute power corrupts absolutely." To which we add: *Power always accumulates unless the power grabbers are stopped!*

The larger the government, the more powerful it becomes. This is an inescapable fact. It doesn't matter how it became larger, or whether the motivation of the people who added to its size was malevolent or benevolent. In the end, it becomes corrupt.

Accumulation of power leads to the diminishing of power somewhere else. In other words, additional power in government means less power for individuals over life, property, and business. As individuals lose power, it is grabbed by government. And ultimately, each one of us loses his ability to run his own life.

If the rules come from outside our country as a result of *international* agreements, then the ability of the individual to have any say over his life, liberty, and business is even more impaired, if not gone completely.

In this case, the individual will have next to a zero chance of altering his condition.

It is hard enough for the individual to affect local city or town government, harder still at the state level, and nearly impossible at the federal level. Imagine a world where the individual or a business faces a world system.

The Trans-Pacific Partnership negotiations, even though held in tight secrecy, are known through leaks to have only 5 of the 29 chapters in the first draft that deal with actual trade. The other chapters seek to impose more regulations about non-trade policies, including incentives to move American industry offshore — similar to what happened with NAFTA.

As government grows, it assumes *and then demands* even more rights held by the people over life, property, business, and liberty itself. Our Constitution was crafted to prevent this. In fact, our Declaration of Independence asserts that our rights come from our Creator. They are not given to us by government nor can they be legitimately taken away from us by government.

The Founders of the United States understood these principles. They framed the Constitution to limit government power through a system of checks and balances coupled with strict limits on what government was authorized to do. Then they added the Bill of Rights to assure that certain rights were protected.

Our government was instituted to guarantee that the people retain their independence, both as individuals and as a people united under a limited federal government. The entire function of our government in the beginning was to protect individual God-given rights, such as life, liberty, and property. In a word: freedom.

Some rights were not enumerated since they were understood to exist universally. These were deeply ingrained in the minds of the people, such as the right of life and the right to own property. Our Founders never imagined that the people would allow these two fundamental rights to be abrogated.

Powerful Government Always Ignores the Rights of the People

What is happening today is something some very clever men promoted in the mid-1800s, and even earlier; men who wanted an international government and meant to run it. They didn't achieve their final goal during their lifetimes, but others have followed their plan and, sad to say, these persons are getting closer and closer to success.

We are referring specifically to Karl Marx and Frederick Engels. Marx had clearly indicated that free trade was an important step in their design since it breaks down the old social order. He "forgot" to say what he had in mind to replace it with when he stated on January 9, 1848 in Brussels, Belgium:

> Free trade breaks up old nationalities.... In a word, the free trade system hastens social revolution.

One month later, *The Communist Manifesto* came off the presses. What Marx "forgot" to say in Brussels was included in the *Manifesto*. Written by Marx and Engels, this document repeatedly attacks property rights; it even bluntly calls for the "abolition" of private property. Marx and Engels stated that as economic conditions worsen because of such attacks, the people who experience the pinch will demand that the government "do something." But the "something" government does would make matters worse and lead to the breakdown of freedom on the way to world government.

Here is how they outlined the communist/socialist strategy. (Keep in mind that both communists and socialists claim Marx as their leader and his works as theirs). The Marxian strategy calls for programs that are far from harmless — deliberately harmful in fact — and these gradually reach dangerous levels of government power on the way to achieving the Marxist goal of total government. The *Manifesto* states:

> In the beginning, this cannot be effected except by means of despotic inroads on the rights of property, and on the means of bourgeois production; by means of measures, therefore, which appear economically insufficient and untenable, but which in the course of the movement, outstrip themselves, necessitate further inroads upon the old social order, and are unavoidable as means of entirely revolutionizing the mode of production.

Note that having already pronounced their complete antipathy to the very concept of private property in previous passages, Marx and Engels tell of their plan to force "despotic inroads on the rights of property" that will worsen the conditions of the people. Finally, widespread agony and disillusionment will present the government with an opportunity to institute "further inroads" and impose the desired result, that of "entirely revolutionizing" what once was freedom.

This has been the pattern with many initiatives created by government, and it is certainly obvious with so-called free trade agreements. They start out looking as though they will solve domestic economic problems, yet they produce more problems. The solution then offered is more government or, currently, more international agreements.

This cycle will lead to a loss of freedom for the people unless the people realize that the real solution is to go back to what was enjoyed prior to the trade agreements. In other words, cancel them. This is a difficult course to promote, but not an insurmountable one. It must be adopted before an all-powerful government is instituted that could stop the voices of the people and lead them to a condition of totally lost freedom.

It is that, or embroiling ourselves in more entangling alliances that will erode all of our freedoms. One or the other, the choice is really yours to make while you have the time.

We ask again: What is wrong with simply allowing free businessmen (producers) to work out their own arrangements and conduct business without government regulating and taxing them into oblivion? If some country won't allow our businessmen to work with their businessmen, then perhaps we shouldn't do business with businesses in that country at all. It is a clue that such a country is corrupt and/or operates under a system of socialism.

To negotiate agreements with such regimes and

meet somewhere in the middle, so to speak, means giving up something in order to make an agreement. That something will always equate to the loss of liberty for our people and a departure from our form of government.

If you are not familiar with the socialist mindset, they hate free enterprise. Every move they make, every agreement they enter into, every compromise, is designed to move any capitalist system at least a step toward socialism. You cannot separate this idea from them any more than you can remove the bones from a hand and expect it to function.

Some socialists work with patient gradualism; others are militant to the point of violence. Regardless of the method they employ, they all agree on the elimination of free enterprise.

Yes, resisting the lure of foreign trade with some foreigners and their governments could well mean the loss of business within the United States. But this is already happening as a result of recent free trade agreements. There are fewer and fewer small and medium-sized businesses. Many of these businesses have been swallowed up by giant conglomerates that milk them for a while and then turn to importing all they offer to consumers. Producers have either gone out of business because they can't compete with imports or have relocated overseas to remain in business. With these relocations, jobs have gone away.

It is of course true that trade pacts are not wholly blameworthy for this frightening development, but they have surely contributed to the problem.

If we had a balance of imports and exports, we would have less of a problem than we do. From an economic aspect, this is self-evident. With an imbalance of more imports than exports, it hurts our economy. It not only hurts our economy, it provides the opportunity for a very dangerous situation to develop regarding our very security. (See Chapter Seven — Homeland Security)

The Transatlantic Trade and Investment Partnership

The latest proposal designed to immerse the United States in a world system is the Transatlantic Trade and Investment Partnership. It has sometimes been referred to as the TTIP.

Backers of the TTIP include numerous business and political leaders who either do not understand what this type of agreement truly leads to, or are themselves closet partisans for an eventual socialistic world government. If the TTIP is approved by Congress, there can be little doubt that, like NAFTA and other "free trade" pacts already entered into, businessmen will lose their ability to function independently, the U.S. economy will suffer even more, and our nation's sovereignty established by the U.S. Constitution will be further eroded.

Let us address what many ask about the businessmen who advocate such agreements and endorse and even finance the march toward socialism. The questions frequently posed are: How can businessmen do such things? Are they not advocates of free enterprise? Do they not know that socialism will destroy their businesses?

Answers to such questions vary. However, in most instances the businessmen noted in the mainstream media are more managers of publicly traded entities than they are entrepreneurs. They do not "own" the businesses they represent. If an array of companies is taken over, they believe that they will still be benefiting from them at a salary level far greater than any worker's. Or, they will receive a separation package that will set them up for life. Furthermore, they have received their education in universities that promote socialism, and most don't realize the wrongness of the instruction they have received. Why would anyone expect them to think any differently than the professors who taught them?

Mass media, universities, think tanks, and government-issued releases make trade agreements seem to be a sure route to full employment and prosperity. Yet, agreements already in place haven't brought about the regularly promised results. Also, these pacts have been made with countries with which trade has always occurred without such so-called free trade agreements.

One obvious example of a consistent U.S. trading partner when no "free trade" pact existed is Canada. Trade was accomplished by U.S. business leaders dealing with their Canadian counterparts. Practically no government interference existed, but gradually as both the Canadian and U.S. governments grew, so did the imposition of trade regulations. And now we have NAFTA, and had it not been for The John Birch Society's campaign to resist plans to build upon NAFTA, our nation would have been placed in a formal North American Union where independence would have been cast aside. (See Chapter Five — An American EU) The history of these so-called free trade agreements is not less government interference but more and more.

Within the public statements are many clues as to what will change. These changes primarily take control out of the hands of our citizens and Congress and subject all to a multiplicity of rules, regulations, and standards.

According to the U.S. Constitution, Congress is authorized to regulate commerce with foreign nations. With the advent of modern trade agreements, this authority has been effectively and unconstitutionally transferred to international bodies.

Many of the trade agreements are supposedly intended to remove or reduce state-run government-supported enterprises competing with American business and products. But even if this were the actual intent of the architects of these agreements, it would break down over time since, with international arbiters, our country possesses only one vote within any agreement. Our American private companies would have to compete with the state-run and state-subsidized enterprises from other countries that send their goods into the United States. Ultimately, in any partnership, our businessmen would have to compete with socialist, government-run factories and governments.

Under such a lopsided condition, it wouldn't be long before the American companies would request government subsidies in order to compete and to stay in operation. But would the trade pacts allow it? Even if they did, does such a turn of events have anything to do with free enterprise?

An example of the problem with private enterprise

competing with state-supported operations is the ongoing struggle between the Boeing Company and Europe's Airbus. Airbus' parent corporation, EADS, is a creation of the governments of the EU forcing the merger of independent and state-operated aerospace industries in Europe. It enjoys the benefits of the EU wanting the business to succeed since it employs tens of thousands of workers all over Europe. Boeing operates under the handicap of working as an independent company. One can argue that Boeing has the benefit of defense contracts, as does EADS, but Boeing does not have the tax benefits and other perks that come with what is really a socialist, government-controlled company.

There is no way that any partnership with Europe would benefit the American aerospace industry if the 28 member states would vote against the one vote of the United States in such a structure. Think about this in terms of future military necessities.

Mexico has 44 bilateral trade agreements with countries all over the world, far more than does the United States. One has to ask the question whether this has helped the Mexican economy or hindered it. Considering the corruption of doing business in Mexico, the answer can reasonably be guessed. Also, if the number of Mexican citizens crossing our southern border looking for work is any indication, these 44 bilateral trade agreements haven't helped Mexico and its average citizens.

Looking at the agreements on the table now, it becomes clear that they are designed to deliberately lead our nation and its people into forming actual partnerships with draconian-style governments. Let us elaborate in the next chapter.

4
The European Union (EU)

The European Union has been portrayed to the American people and certainly to Europeans as a successful path to prosperity and away from any future devastating wars — such as World Wars I and II. The picture painted in America's schools and editorial pages is one of blissful happiness with all the peoples of Europe marching together toward financial success, personal progress, and peaceful foreign relations. This rosy picture at least acknowledges that there have been minor road bumps, but this is to be expected with any new system of government.

The reality is something remarkably different. The EU, in fact, is creating a massively intrusive government over its member states while accumulating power even beyond the European Continent.[3]

Moves toward the European Union started out just

3. While on a visit to Germany in 1990, this author sat in the office of Frank Piplat, the public relations officer for the European Economic Commission (EEC) in Bonn, Germany. At that time, the EEC was transitioning into the more dominant European Community. It was one of the steps leading to the creation of the European Union. Piplat stated that once all of Europe was bound together in the multinational organization being planned, it would be larger than the United States in geography, economic power, and population. After accomplishing this, he said, they would bring the United States into the EU kicking and screaming if necessary. In other words, this "public relations" officer was telling us that America would be forced to give up independence and the U.S. Constitution to become only a cog in the wheel of European socialism. He plainly spelled out this goal and, we might add, he did so quite arrogantly.

after World War II as a relatively small coal and steel agreement among six Western European countries. Only a few observers raised their voices worrying that those who were negotiating this agreement actually had something much larger in mind: the ultimate union of all of Europe into a single state. They were ignored, even ridiculed.

Even as late as 1989, people would not believe what was in store for Europe. In the April 10, 1989 edition of *The New American* magazine, William F. Jasper's article "United States of Europe" stated that, based on agreements then being negotiated, coupled with others already in force, the once-sovereign countries of Europe would be submerged in a supranational state with a centralized European Parliament. Only a few believed his prediction had any merit.

Dr. Ron Paul, who wasn't serving in Congress at the time, warned that the emerging European pact would create a statist system as a huge step toward a world central bank. Likewise, few took his warning seriously.

The forecasts of these two men have proven largely accurate. Progress toward today's EU has been accomplished piecemeal through one agreement after another so that the peoples of Europe didn't become alarmed.

Those who have brought this about are followers of Marx and are members of various socialist parties throughout the region. Countries such as Germany, England, France, Sweden, Norway, Spain, Greece, and others have frequently been in the grip of socialist parties.

When in power, the socialists negotiated the agreements leading to the EU. Occasionally, the people voted the socialists out, but the agreements were not canceled or repealed by new leaders. Just as in the United States, the party of the "outs" has attacked the party of the "ins," even occasionally succeeding in replacing it. But there has been no rolling back of the steady progress toward the Marxist goal.

American armed forces saved Europe from Hitler's National Socialism (Nazism) during World War II and watched as it was replaced by international socialism. Since these socialist parties are all linked to the Socialist International founded by Karl Marx, they have as their primary goal the linkage of all countries into the Marxian socialist worldwide system.

Here we have to recall Mark Twain's comment that fiction alone has to be credible, while reality can actually be incredible. The European Union, when studied diligently, differs greatly from what is taught in our schools and presented by our mass media. Indeed, the reality is quite incredible.

Rather than something new, the dream of a United Europe is quite ancient. Attempts toward unity over the centuries have involved wars of conquest, from the Romans of two millennia ago to Napoleon. All who have tried this have failed. But a new route toward achieving the goal came to life after World War II. Hitler's idea of how to accomplish European unity was championed by his economic minister, Albert Speer, as far back as 1942. It was called the *Europäische Wirtschaftsgemeinschaft.* When translated, this means European Economic Community.

The goal expressed by the Nazi government was one European state, one central bank, and one currency. Thankfully, Hitler lost his battle for a United Europe, but his dream didn't die with him. Socialists who rose to power after Nazism was crushed kept the idea alive. In 1958, 13 years after the death of Nazism, they named their plan the European Economic Community — the same name used by Albert Speer. This incremental step was also informally called the "Common Market."

In 1973, several other nations joined and the name of the increasingly political entanglement became the European Community. When the number of nations grew to 12 in 1986, the European flag began to be used by the Community. The European Union was formally established in 1993 when the Maastricht Treaty went into effect.

It's no secret that the formerly independent countries of the EU have suffered economically. In large part, this has been brought about from socialist benefits handed out to the people to buy their votes. Such monetary policies have come close to collapsing the economy of the more socialist countries — huge deficits in other words. But EU leaders dare not tax the people directly to the extent needed to fulfill their promises.

Rather than bringing prosperity to Europe, the EU has encouraged fiscal irresponsibility. As "partners," the countries know that they will be bailed out and not permitted to go bankrupt and collapse. The politics of the situation demand that the dream of the single European state must be kept alive.

The bailout process only encourages other member nations to be equally irresponsible since they expect that they, too, will be rescued. This house of cards should collapse but it will be buttressed if they find a new rich "partner." Covetous eyes have looked across the sea to the wealthy United States of America.

In the 21st century, a bailout of one EU member has

been followed by similar bailouts of others. America's mass media portrays Germany as Europe's bank of last resort with the ability to finance EU members in trouble. However, the U.S. Federal Reserve came to Europe's rescue. This fact would have never been known had not a relatively superficial audit of the Federal Reserve taken place in 2011. It came after years of pressure from members of Congress to examine the Fed's books.

Even though the partial audit didn't bare all aspects of the Fed's operations, it provided a glimpse into the Fed, which has never been fully audited in its 100-year history, despite its financial control over our economy and monetary system. The word "incredible" surely applies.

Through the magic of "currency exchanges," the Federal Reserve has sent American dollars all over Europe without a vote of Congress or the approval of the American people. Some members of Congress have attempted to prove that the currency exchanges were, in fact, mere cover for Federal Reserve bailouts of EU members and the EU itself. But the secrecy that has always been the hallmark of the Fed has been too tight for anyone to find out the whole truth. Dr. Ron Paul's warning that a world central bank would be created appears to have been right on target, even if it hasn't yet been formalized.

The influence of the Federal Reserve extends to the entire financial world. The June 21, 2013 issue of the *New York Times* quoted Mark Frey of the Canadian-based Cambridge Mercantile Group as saying, "The Fed isn't just the U.S.'s central bank. It's the world's central bank." Looking at the way the Fed bails out foreign entities with American taxpayer monies, it appears that this is the case.

Where is the indignation over these facts by the national media, liberal or conservative?

The fact that the Fed is helping the socialist entities of Europe should come as no surprise because creation of the Federal Reserve was urged in *The Communist Manifesto* as Step #5 on the way to communize any country. Marx and Engels called for "Centralization of credit in the hands of the State, by means of a national bank with State capital and an exclusive monopoly." The Federal Reserve functions in this capacity; many members of Congress have tried to alert citizens to this fact for an entire century, but they have been ridiculed in the press and ignored by most of their colleagues.

What is known of the negotiations leading to the Transatlantic Trade and Investment Partnership indicates that merging the United States with the EU is a key portion of the agreement being crafted by planners on *both sides* of the Atlantic.

The ultimate goal is a one-world government, arrived at one step at a time through any form of foreign entanglement the planners can devise. But the most successful steps are so-called free trade agreements, because the average American businessman supports free trade and doesn't understand what these agreements really do to our economy and his ability to function as an independent businessman. And the average American, if he or she becomes even curious about the EU, does not comprehend *how these trade agreements affect our constitutional system and national independence.*

In addition, since the edicts and regulations from foreign entanglements are implemented by the federal bureaucracy, the federal government gets the blame and the businessman does not see the connection to any agreement or treaty.

In the Pacific, the Chinese Communist government is forming more and more pacts with Western states, including the EU. Its officials are using expertise gained from exporting goods to the United States while they implement plans toward additional mergers.

A May 23, 2013 article published by AFP, the French news agency, reported that the Chinese were forming a free trade deal with Switzerland (not a member of the EU). It pointed out that for China to negotiate with the EU, it would have to deal with the (then) 27-state bloc, not just individual states. It further stated that, in dealing with the Swiss, the talks will include negotiations not only on economic issues but on such areas as finance, the environment, human rights, and international security. Here is confirmation of the fact that these pacts cover far more than trade.

Unbeknownst to most Americans, the states that comprise the EU are led not only by socialists but by so-called ex-communists. The book *Das Erste Leben der Angela M.* (*The First Life of Angela M.*) exposes the fact that German leader Angela Merkel was an enthusiastic communist earlier in her life. She is not the first "former" communist to rise to the post of Germany's chancellor. Even when Germany was split East and West, it was public knowledge that supposedly anti-communist West Germany was led by a leader in the Socialist International named Willy Brandt. After he left office, it became known that he was actually an East German communist secret police agent.[4]

Forming partnerships with socialists of any stripe is not in the best interest of the United States. Should the EU make a deal with Communist China, how would that affect the United States should our country form a *partnership* with the EU?

In a speech he delivered in England in 2000, unrepentant former Soviet dictator Mikhail Gorbachev referred to the EU as "the new European Soviet." He added that it would become a "common European home" and that it would eventually include Russia and all of the nations that had been dominated by the former USSR. Vladimir Bukovsky, the famous Russian dissident who survived years of confinement and torture in Soviet prisons, labeled the EU "a monster" that must be dismantled before it becomes a dictatorship like the one he opposed in his native Russia.

Yet, warnings from Bukovsky and others in Europe were ignored, just as warnings were similarly ignored in America. In 2003, Czech President Vaclav Klaus stated that a proposed EU Constitution "would mean no more

4. During the period when East and West Germany were being reunited in the wake of the apparent collapse of the Soviet communism, this author had a conversation with a member of the West German Cabinet. He expressed his concern over the fact that the East German government never had a de-Nazification program inside the civil service, such as happened in West Germany. He was concerned because the reuniting of the two parts of Germany would give posts to both East German communists and older Nazis.

sovereign states in Europe ... only one state will remain." Two years later, British authors Christopher Booker and Richard North released their extensively documented book *The Great Deception: The Secret History of the European Union*. It described the EU as "a slow-motion coup d'état, the most spectacular coup d'état in all history."

In 2004, United Kingdom Independence Party official Mike Nattrass stated:

> The EU was sold to the British people *as a trading agreement* and has turned into a political union which is changing our basic laws and traditions. [Emphasis added.]

Bernard Connolly, a former senior official in the European Commission, lamented:

> It has now become clear to us that *what we thought was a Common Market* is nothing more than a project to create a European federal super-state in which our sovereignty, Britain's national identity, would be extinguished. [Emphasis added.]

By June 2004, EU membership had grown to 25. Its

leaders produced a constitution for the EU proclaiming it to have "primacy over the law of member states." In turn, this document explicitly noted the EU's subservience to the United Nations. Not only were the nations of Europe subordinating themselves to a European Union, the EU "constitution" was subordinating itself in turn to the UN.

Member nations within the EU were supposed to approve the 2004 constitution but, once the voters in both France and the Netherlands registered emphatic disapproval, the approval process changed. England's leaders refused to allow the British people the referendum they had been promised because of certainty that it would indicate more disapproval of the EU.

English EU Parliament member Daniel Hannan, a well-known EU opponent, claimed that those rejections of the EU Constitution by voters in France and the Netherlands were essentially meaningless. He stated:

> You may have got the impression that the European Constitution was dead — that the French had felled it and the Dutch had pounded a stake into its heart. If so, think again. The Constitution is being implemented, clause by clause as if the No votes had not happened.

Without being able to achieve the required unanimous consent required for approval of the new constitution, EU leaders scrapped their plan to gain approval for it by means of national referendums, and *recast their proposal as a "treaty."* Its ratification was gained, not by the parliaments or the voters in nation after nation, but by socialist leaders of each formerly independent nation when they gathered in Lisbon in 2007. That was the same year that Roman Herzog, Germany's president 1994-1999, pointed out that "84 percent of the legal acts in Germany stemmed from [EU headquarters in] Brussels." The EU continues to dominate the nations that have submitted to its rule.

And, it was all done by hiding what the planners had in store. In a revealing interview in *La Stampa* on July 13, 2000, Italian Prime Minister Giuliano Amato, who later became vice-president of the EU Constitutional Convention, stated:

> One must act *"as if"* in Europe: *as if one wanted only very few things, in order to obtain a great deal. As if nations were to remain sovereign, in order to convince them to surrender their sovereignty.* The Commission in Brussels, for example, must act as if it were a technical organism,

in order to operate like a government ... and so on, camouflaging and toning down. The sovereignty lost at the national level does not pass to any new subject. It is entrusted to a faceless entity: NATO, and the UN and eventually the EU. The Union is the vanguard of this changing world: it indicates a future of Princes without sovereignty. The new entity is faceless and those who are in command can neither be pinned down nor elected.... That is the way Europe was made too: by creating communitarian organisms without giving the organism presided over by national governments the impression that they are being subjected to a higher power.

That is how the Court of Justice as a supra-national organ was born. It was a sort of unseen atom bomb, which Robert Schuman and Jean Monnet slipped into the negotiations on the Coal and Steel Community. That was what the "CSC" itself was: a random mixture of national egotisms which became communitarian. *I don't think it is a good idea to replace this slow and effective method — which keeps national States free from anxiety while they are being stripped of power — with great institutional leaps. Therefore*

> *I prefer to go slowly, to crumble pieces of sover-*
> *eignty up little by little,* avoiding brusque transi-
> tions from national to [EU] federal power. That
> is the way I think we will have to build Europe's
> common policies.... [Emphasis added.]

Here in America, significant support for the proposed
TTIP is virtually certain among approximately 80 members of our Congress who are members of the Social
Democrats. (They refer to themselves as something else
when they run for office. In other words, they too hide
what they have as goals for the American people as they
move slowly toward their goal.)

How many senators are Social Democrats isn't
known. But what is known is that the organization
labeled Social Democrats is the official representative in
the United States to the Socialist International, the
worldwide group started by Karl Marx before he passed
into eternity in 1883.[5]

At this point, some readers will conclude that this
book seeks to prove that a conspiracy is at work and that
what has been presented is the work of that conspiracy.
Such a conclusion is regularly pooh-poohed by the mass

5. The Internet supplies information about House members who are identified as members of
the Social Democrats. Look up Social Democrats in Congress. Of the 80, 70 have openly
acknowledged this affiliation, but the mass media has never revealed it to the public.

media as extremist hysteria, but more people are beginning to sense that one exists. Remember, pointing to Hitler's rise to power was characterized as a "conspiracy theory" until Nazism became *conspiracy fact* in Europe. By then, it was too late to stop him and his collection of criminals, and armed might became necessary.

There are even more problems with existing pacts, such as sustainable development rules that are required in American communities through adoption of UN programs aimed at local governments. These stem from the UN's *Agenda 21*. (See Chapter Eight — *Agenda 21*) All of these entanglements result in compromising national sovereignty and diminishing the ability of Americans to use their property as they see fit — for recreation, business, mining, manufacturing, etc.

Many more international agreements are imposing environmental rules and regulations on our country even though they have been rejected by Congress. Most of these emanate from pacts entered into with the United Nations. Bit by bit and in the name of "sustainable development," rules and regulations are being created that have little to do with the stated purpose of the various pacts.

No Borders

One of the key provisions of the agreements that formed the European Union is that there would be no borders separating the countries. People could come and go as they please. Libertarians were delighted, but the new arrangement quickly turned into a system whereby those from less fortunate countries could move en masse to the more affluent countries, where they could not only seek employment but obtain various forms of welfare.

To some this may appear to be wonderful, but it turned out to have negative consequences, especially for those who have long been their country's workforce. Imagine what would occur if a similar situation were established between the United States and Mexico. Yet this was one of the desired consequences of the 2005 Security and Prosperity Partnership. Once the light of day was shone on the SPP and the designs of its creators to lead our country into a North American Union were sufficiently exposed, its name was changed.

The SPP is now the North American Leaders' Summit and the same goals are being sought. Had they been successfully achieved, the floodgates of migration from Latin America into the United States would have been opened. There would no longer be any restrictions on movement over what was once a national border. And polling has shown that at least one-third of the people in Mexico would like to relocate to the United States.

Consider the following example of what happened when free movement of people within the European Union became the rule. Keep in mind that this is what could happen here.

Partnerships mean that rules must be uniform. Recent moves by Great Britain to free herself from EU regulations have demonstrated that, once entangled in one of these partnerships, a formerly free nation becomes powerless. The May 31, 2013 *New York Times* published an article reporting that the EU was seeking to force Britain to provide social security, child support, and other benefits to newly arrived foreign citizens, simply because they are citizens of one of the formerly independent EU nations. These are people who want to move into Great Britain from other countries to enjoy a better life than they had in their former country. Why wouldn't they relocate to Britain? But British citizens don't want to support newly arriving foreigners who have not contributed to the system and have relocated to get in on the dole — at their expense.

EU rules and regulations have even extended to the tolls charged by France and England for using the "Chunnel" under the English Channel. The countries at both ends of the Chunnel decided on fees that cover the cost of maintaining it, but the EU sued both countries to lower the tolls in order to attract more people to use it.

Imagine the formation of a partnership between our nation and the EU. The proposed Transatlantic Trade and Investment Partnership would create an arrangement between the EU and USA like the one that has entangled Great Britain. Significantly, President Barack Obama publicly warned Britain to stay in the EU because the United States would not make a free trade agreement with the UK separately. So, while public sentiment in England has been turning against membership in the EU, our president has been pressuring Britain to remain entangled.

Finally, regarding the formation of a partnership with the EU, if the EU reaches a point where it experiences a wide scale financial collapse — not simply a number of individual states but the Union itself — the Federal Reserve will come to its rescue and there will be additional pressure to drag America into the EU. There are very few signs that EU nations have learned anything when it comes to fiscal responsibility. After all, what can be expected of socialistic governments and socialist leaders?

5
An American EU

Soon after taking office in 2001, President George W. Bush announced his plan to have the United States lead in the formation of the Free Trade Area of the Americas (FTAA). His goal called for having 34 nations of the Western Hemisphere (all except Cuba) unite in a virtual duplication of the European Union. He added that its provisions would be carefully negotiated, presented to Congress by 2005, and fully operational by the year 2010.

Opposition to this scheme, led by a massive effort conducted by The John Birch Society and by resolutions of several state legislatures prompted by JBS members, succeeded in blocking creation of the FTAA.

The Bush administration then began promoting the less ambitious Security and Prosperity Partnership (SPP). He was joined in that effort by the leaders of Canada and Mexico. On March 23, 2005 the SPP was launched in Waco, Texas. Mr. Bush stood alongside Canadian leader Paul Martin and Mexico's leader

Vicente Fox to announce their new agreement. This initiative so obviously called for North American integration that it made strikingly transparent plans to create a North American Union (NAU).

Even before he participated in the creation of the SPP, Mexico's President Fox had stated on May 16, 2002:

> Eventually our long-range objective is to establish with the United States ... an ensemble of connections and institutions similar to those created by the European Union.

That does not sound like free trade or prosperity, but it does sound like partnership and a call for terminating the independence of Mexico, Canada, and the United States.

On May 27, 2010, Mexico's President Felipe Calderon stated:

> Integration is key to restoring strong sustained growth in North America.... We need more integration, not isolation, not protectionism.

Here, the openly stated goal is more than free trade. It is, as he said, "integration." Again, it is a partnership that would transfer American national power into a single international entity. Independence would become a relic of the past.

Anyone who accessed the official SPP website (SPP. gov) before it was taken down could have seen very clearly that the aim of these leaders included integration of police, armed forces, banking, environmental regulations, healthcare, and more. Especially noteworthy was its *elimination of existing borders*. As difficult as this might be to believe, it is nonetheless true.

There were voices who tried to convince others in and out of government that the goals of this program were a myth, or at least not dangerous. Skeptics who refused to believe The John Birch Society's claims about the SPP's true purpose changed their tune once they visited SPP.gov. What they found was even worse than what JBS members were telling them.

The SPP's end goal was formation of a new country through merger, abandoning the independence of the three nations, scrapping the U.S. Constitution (and the constitutions of the two neighboring countries), and setting up a new government to rule the three former nations. All of this was supposedly necessary to guarantee security and prosperity. Further, the new system included opening up trade (a lure for the unwary), but this would be accompanied by a total breakdown of our economy, and open borders to allow foreign citizens to migrate into the United States to compete with our businessmen and to compete with our citizens for jobs.

But it was sold, and is being sold, as free trade — a smokescreen that hides a sovereignty-destroying trap! All one has to consider in order to see that it is a trap is: 1) trade among the three nations has existed for centuries and there is no need for a new relationship; and 2) reading the document and the attitudes of those who signed it shows that the goal is merger, not just more business deals.

In May 2005, two months after the creation of the SPP, the Council on Foreign Relations issued a 175-page book entitled *Building a North American Community*. Its chief author was CFR member Robert Pastor, and it carried a foreword written by CFR President Richard N. Haass. The book called for "the establishment by 2010 of a North American economic and security community." It further recommended harmonizing the borders; free passage for all within the three nations; a new "security perimeter" that would encircle Canada, the United States, and Mexico; and more.

There are a number of important points that must be considered in response to these recommendations by the CFR and the leaders of the three countries.

First, it is next to impossible for any organization to

64

write, edit, compile, publish, and put into circulation a book in two months — especially one that possesses the kind of detail present in *Building a North American Community*. It is hardly excessive to conclude that CFR leaders knew about the plans for a North American Union well in advance, or were the planners behind it from the beginning.

The Council on Foreign Relations was established to promote a one-world government after the U.S. Senate defeated a move to involve the United States in the League of Nations after World War I. It is still actively working toward a one-world government today, and has played a prominent role in establishing the United Nations and maintaining a U.S. foreign policy of subordination to the UN.

Second, a new security perimeter would mean cooperation with and integration of military and policing forces of the three countries. Supposedly needed to lessen the danger of terrorist attacks, the expanded border would enclose all three countries — with no border between the three countries.

Third, and more importantly, the problem at our border with illegal immigrants continuing to cross into the U.S. hasn't been dealt with because the men in government and their powerful allies in organizations such

George Washington:
"The great rule of conduct for us, in regard to foreign nations is, in extending our commercial relations, to have with them as little political connection as possible."

Thomas Jefferson:
"I deem [one of] the essential principles of our government [to be] peace, commerce, and honest friendship with all nations, entangling alliances with none...."

Henry Kissinger addresses the third annual Washington Ideas Forum at the Newseum in Washington on October 6, 2011. Back on July 18, 1993, he wrote an Op-Ed article for the *Los Angeles Times* under the headline, "With NAFTA, U.S. Finally Creates a New World Order." In this article he wrote, "Before the end of summer, President Bill Clinton will ask Congress to approve the North American Free Trade Agreement.... It will represent the most creative step toward a new world order taken by any group of countries since the end of the Cold War, and the first step toward the even larger vision of a free-trade zone for the entire Western Hemisphere."

With NAFTA, U.S. Finally Creates a New World Order

■ **Trade:** Mexico is going to be the most important neighbor in U.S. history. With this pact, its path on the road to democracy and openness will be assured.

By Henry A. Kissinger

NEW YORK

Before the end of summer, President Bill Clinton will ask Congress to approve the North American Free Trade Agreement, linking the Unit-

next century—with or without NAFTA. By then it will be a country with a population of more than 100 million and equal to the Asian "little tigers," such as Korea. Our de facto open borders make friendly relations a vital national interest. Twenty-million Mexican residents in the United States link the interests of the two nations on the human level. The healthier Mexico's economy, the lower the illegal immigration and the greater U.S. exports will be to an economy whose propensity to import from us is the highest in the world.

Even on strictly economic grounds,

Why doesn't the government of Mexico think enough of its own citizens to work toward a system that allows the average Mexican to succeed? Instead, Mexico's leaders actually encourage illegal immigration into the United States — shoving their problems across the border. The evidence of this fact is there for all to see, including the outrageous printing of comic-book style instructions entitled *Guía Del Migrante Mexicano* (Guide for the Mexican Migrant) by the Mexican government to show their own citizens how to cross into the United States and meld into the American society.

www.cfif.org

AP Images

Newt Gingrich (R-Ga.) meets reporters at Capitol Hill in Washington on May 12, 1994. Gingrich sought the immersion of our government into the WTO even though he warned about its power during his testimony before the House Ways and Means Committee in June 1994. He told his colleagues, "I am just saying that we need to be honest about the fact that we are transferring from the United States at a practical level significant authority to a new organization. This is a transformational moment." In a lame-duck session of Congress later that year, he then voted for what he had warned others about.

In an impressive display of Council on Foreign Relations (CFR) domination of the Departments of State and Defense. President George W. Bush paused for a photograph on Thursday, January 5, 2006, with present and former Secretaries of State and Defense in the Oval Office at the White House. As of that year, everyone in the photo except Bush were current (14) or former (2) CFR members. Bush met with the bipartisan group to discuss the war in Iraq. From left is former Secretary of Defense Harold Brown, former Secretary of State Lawrence Eagleburger, former Secretary of State James Baker, former Secretary of State Colin Powell, former Secretary of Defense James Schlesinger, Secretary of Defense Donald Rumsfeld, Vice President Dick Cheney, Bush, Secretary of State Condoleezza Rice, former Secretary of State George Schultz, former Secretary of Defense Melvin Laird, former Secretary of State Madeleine Albright, former Secretary of State Alexander Haig, former Secretary of Defense Robert McNamara, former Secretary of Defense William Perry, and former Secretary of Defense William Cohen.

Former President George H.W. Bush speaks at a dedication ceremony for the George and Barbara Bush Center at the University of New England, Friday, October 3, 2008, in Biddeford, Maine. Back in August 1991, Mr. Bush made the creation of a New World Order, by that name, an official policy of the government of the United States. The State Department issued his proclamation in a document entitled National Security Strategy of the United States. The preface, titled "A NEW WORLD ORDER," is signed by George H. W. Bush, a completely unconstitutional act.

Dr. Robert A. Pastor, professor of international relations and director of the Center for North American Studies at American University speaks in Panama City, Panama, Monday, July 31, 2006. In his latest book, *The North American Idea: A Vision of a Continental Future* (2012), Pastor specifically names "The John Birch Society" as among the leading groups that "have been the most vocal, active and intense on North American issues, and they were effective in inhibiting the Bush administration and deterring the Obama administration from any grand initiatives."

Canada's Prime Minister Paul Martin, right, Mexico's President Vicente Fox, left, and U.S. President George W. Bush, center, are shown following their meetings and a joint news conference at Baylor University in Waco, Texas, Wednesday, March 23, 2005, where they announced the formation of the Security and Prosperity Partnership of North America, a steppingstone to the North American Union.

United Nations Headquarters, New York City

Don't be fooled into believing that proponents of world government are trying to establish something that will benefit mankind. The end result they seek will be bigger governments that are totally separated from the individual; governments in which the voter will have minimal influence, if any. And their goal will be a world government in which the United States will merely be one among many. As we write, there are 193 member nations in the UN. And the veto our nation possesses as a permanent member of the UN Security Council remains in the hands of U.S. leaders who, far from resisting the UN's stealthy progression toward total power, applaud this ominous development and pose no threat to it being finalized.

as the CFR don't want to solve it. What they desire is no borders and the free flow of people as if there are no geographic and/or political constraints. The SPP called for a partnership, not independent action. It was a step toward a North American copy of the EU.

Thankfully, due to efforts waged primarily by members of The John Birch Society, approximately 36 state legislatures considered resolutions against this scheme. If the problem had not been real, these legislative bodies would never have given it the time of day.

Meanwhile, the average American had no idea that a battle was even raging behind the scenes to save the United States as an independent nation. The mass media continued to ignore the threat. Mentions of either the entire scheme or a mere portion of it were followed by the charge that the scheme was merely a "conspiracy theory" unworthy of respectability. No one was encouraged to look further into the matter. This attitude dominated the media and even some conservative commentators on television. This opinion was also spread by some "respectable" conservative organizations in and around Washington's Beltway.

After the successful effort that blocked creation of the NAU, the project went into a sort of hibernation. Once Barack Obama became president, the SPP became reinvigorated with its new name, the North American Leaders' Summit (NALS), making it appear that any gatherings of the three leaders is nothing more than a get-together to discuss matters of mutual interest. But, not surprisingly, NALS is now promoting creation of the North American Union.

Recent moves illustrate that the same process that led to the creation of the EU is being employed on this side of the Atlantic to create the North American Union.

There are domestic issues such as ObamaCare that fit perfectly with the scheme to create the NAU, though at first glance no relationship would seem to exist. A socialist system of medical care is needed to comfortably merge with countries that have socialized medicine. Free enterprise and socialism are incompatible and we see no movement in Canada or other Western countries to phase out socialized medicine. What we do see is our government doing what it can to build a socialized medical system. To merge medical care, the systems must be similar.

Other sectors of American society and government undergoing changes that will facilitate future merger include banking, law enforcement, environmental regulations, military pacts, etc. All of these aspects of society must become similar or sufficiently controlled in order for the United States to ease into a merger with the NAU and/or EU.

An agreement during the Obama administration formalized permission for Canadian and Mexican armed forces to enter the United States during a national emergency, whether caused by nature or civil unrest. This pact was created at the inaugural Trilateral Meeting of North American Defense Ministers on March 27, 2012 in Ottawa, Canada. The agreement amounts to a first small step toward merging the armed forces of the three countries. Its provisions were not enough to set off alarms among the general public, but it surely should be viewed as alarming by those who truly know what is being sought.

Inviting foreign troops into America for other than training associated with weaponry purchased by their mother country has not happened in all of our history.

By 2013, there were indications of a desire on the part of some leaders to place police in the United States into United Nations programs. On April 5, 2013, *The New American's* website published an article entitled "Baltimore Police Major Attending UN 'Peacekeeping' Course." The opening paragraph reads:

A major with the Baltimore Police Department

will be attending a United Nations "Police Commanders Course" ... in Sweden next week that is raising eyebrows among Americans — especially considering the UN's history and highly controversial agenda. The three-week course is aimed at teaching officers from around the world about "peacekeeping" operations, *interpretation of UN "mandates,"* how to work effectively with international military forces, and more.... [Emphasis added.]

Canada and Mexico maintain *national* control over their police. In the United States, *local* control over the police sets our nation apart and keeps the important role of police from being used against the people. Therefore, the idea of sending local police to any UN training session must be viewed as a dangerous step toward establishing a national — or international — police force in our country.

The importance of retaining control over police departments at the local level cannot be overemphasized. It can be the difference between freedom and despotic government, since dictatorships in modern times have regularly been sustained with a centralized, national police system.

The original timetable for a merger of the three countries through the SPP/NAU process called for completion of these steps by 2010. A massive effort waged primarily by The John Birch Society slowed this initiative to the degree that there wasn't even any talk about it in 2010. Literally millions of pieces of literature were distributed, augmented by the widespread distribution of videos, the giving of numerous speeches, making a large number of radio and television appearances, and countless person-to-person contacts. Especially important were local-level meetings with legislators and opinion molders.

All of these efforts created a groundswell of curiosity and indignation, with the result that the SPP.gov website disappeared from the Internet. Reading what had been posted readily confirmed what members of The John Birch Society were saying. But the effort to compromise U.S. independence and merge the three North American nations continues forward under a new name, and without a website.

Changing the names of targeted groups and eliminating their websites makes obsolete all of the literature, videos, etc., created to expose their schemes. This is only one of the tactics employed by their proponents to diminish the effectiveness of opponents. It also makes more difficult the average citizen's grasp of what is truly occurring.

Keep in mind that SPP.gov was an official website of the U.S. government. It confirmed charges being made that an official goal of our own government included working toward cancelation of U.S. independence by tying our nation to an international entity. After that website disappeared, opponents' literature directing readers to go to the website became obsolete.

By eliminating the website, the internationalists seeking to compromise, even destroy sovereignty for the United States, sought to cover their tracks. Thankfully, in this case, enough of the pages of the website SPP.gov have been archived to show what was stated by this government program.[6]

It is hardly an exaggeration to conclude that massive immigration over recent years has significantly hurt this country economically and culturally. Certainly, handouts provided to illegal immigrants have cost state and local governments dearly and made the states more dependent on federal agencies. The states of Arizona

---

6. SPP website pages are archived at: archive.is/www.spp.gov. This site contains most of the pages that did appear on the SPP.gov website, but it does not include the summary page list of the major segments of society that the SPP claimed would be integrated, such as police, banking, environmental regulations, healthcare, etc. There are several sites that attack the SPP online, but use caution since a few, here and there, use charges against the SPP that are a stretch. The truth is bad enough.

and California have spent huge amounts (as much as $2,000 to $3,000 annually per family!) because of illegal immigration and its ramifications. The taxes collected to pay for the handouts aren't direct, so the average household doesn't see the linkage of state spending and illegal immigration. But the people who are affected know that their taxes keep going up.

In Arizona, the federal government has done all it can to prevent the state from solving its statewide illegal immigrant problem. The people of Arizona are forced to continue the government handouts, and even suffer the cost and consequences of the crime wave generated by the illegals.

These problems will be multiplied tenfold if progress toward an NAU and/or a TTIP continues. Control over government benefits will be lost because of entering a "partnership" similar to what the people of Britain now face.

The John Birch Society believes in the freedom of people to come and go as they please and to settle wherever and whenever they choose. But this must be done legally and with a certain amount of restraint to prevent hordes of people literally invading our country.

There are those who endorse unlimited immigration in the names of freedom and compassion. One portion of their argument claims that borders are not actual geographic boundaries. They insist that borders are artificial and should never be a barrier to the free flow of people. But what they leave out is that borders are political boundaries separating political systems and cultures as much as they do people. The boundaries we have established protect our American system and way of life. Without them, our system will collapse — which is the hidden goal behind unlimited immigration promoted by some who want our system to be altered and merged with other nations.

Nineteenth century British statesman Richard Cobden said it well:

> Peace will come to this earth when her peoples
> have as much as possible to do with each other;
> their governments the least possible.

His wisdom should be listened to. He wasn't a partisan for no government (anarchy), only a partisan for a minimum amount of government. Likewise, The John Birch Society believes that government should have the power to create regulations regarding immigration. Opening the borders to allow entry to large numbers of people who do not understand our system of government will lead to changing the American way from a constitutional Republic into something similar to what they fled.

Further, millions of recent immigrants who don't understand the value of limited government won't choose to elect constitutionalists who seek office. Indeed, there are a multitude of interlocking community action groups, immigrant groups, and religious institutions financed by foundations and the federal government working to organize illegal as well as legal immigrants into a voting bloc for the Left. This has been a continuing problem regardless of which political party occupies the White House.[7]

In regard to immigration, ask yourself the question: Would a hundred million immigrants alter our American system and way of life? What would be the tipping-point of change — 50 million? We are dangerously close to that number now if we combine the numbers of legal and illegal immigrants. The problem is that no one knows for sure. Illegals do not fill out our census forms.

The Pew Research Center has published a report indicating that over 40 million immigrants currently reside in the United States. And the typically cited number of illegal immigrants has not changed since at least

7. Go to the Internet and search for "Aztlan" to learn what is really going on in the illegal immigrant community. You will find its goals eye-opening. Wikipedia alone will not be adequate; further digging will be needed to gain an accurate understanding.

2007: eleven million. This is impossible, and is another example of immigration statistics not being honest.

Also, we cannot simply open the borders and allow unemployed foreigners to become an additional burden on the American taxpayer.

Promoters of open borders have done a good job creating sympathy for illegal immigrants by employing a combination of libertarianism and humanitarianism. But no such thinking can alter the fact that massive illegal immigration is a costly and destructive path for America.

Ironically, Mexico's leaders preach to Americans that we must welcome illegal immigrants into our country with full benefits, while they treat immigrants in their own country as people who have no rights whatsoever.

At best, the government in Mexico is socialist. It is not unusual for open communists to hold posts in the Mexican Cabinet, a fact that is relatively unknown to the American people. This begs a serious question: Why doesn't the government of Mexico think enough of its own citizens to work toward a system that allows the average Mexican to succeed? Instead, Mexico's leaders actually encourage illegal immigration into the United States — shoving their problems across the border. The evidence of this fact is there for all to see, including the outrageous printing of comic-book style instructions by the Mexican government to show their own citizens how to cross into the United States and meld into the American society.

This is the attitude of one of the countries with which our leaders want to form a political partnership.

There are a myriad of public and private organizations in the United States promoting various agreements that lead to world government. They focus on free trade, environmentalism, education, banking, health, population control, agricultural regulations, and much more. We could fill pages with the names of organizations promoting globalism. All of their efforts, of course, lead ultimately to domination of all mankind by the United Nations.

One infuriating aspect of all of this is that money flows out of the United States into many nations and into the United Nations and its many agencies, while controls and regulations come back into the United States as the result of the UN's acquisition of more and more power. Some of the growing clout of the UN comes from the work of the Security Council or the General Assembly, but also from the scores of commissions, organizations, and alphabetized agencies spawned by the UN.

In other words, the world gets the American people's

tax money in foreign aid, dues and special assessments provided to the various UN entities, and bailouts emanating from the Federal Reserve. In return, the world is increasingly telling America what to do and how to operate. This insidious process is so well camouflaged that the average American has no awareness of what is occurring.

All of it raises an important question: If our government keeps financing the UN and many nations that continue to vote against the interests of the American people within the UN, what is the real motivation behind the transfer of all these funds?

Constitutionally minded representatives in Congress have long complained that most of their colleagues support UN "recommendations," as if they are required to do so without any regard to the Constitution or the wishes of their constituents. Only when sufficiently intense grassroots activity points to and protests this process do congressmen listen. Much, however, never comes to the attention of the voters.

6
A Grand Deception

As we have already noted, organizations and national officials advocating merger with other countries or groups of countries like the EU have employed trade agreements as the recommended first step toward world government.

It doesn't take too long to comprehend the breadth and depth of the dilemma facing Americans once you start to surf the Internet for organizations that support the UN: World Federalists, Council on Foreign Relations, Trilateral Commission, Atlantic Council, United Nations Association, Transatlantic Policy Network, Local Governments for Sustainability (ICLEI; formerly known as International Council for Local Environmental Initiatives), and numerous others *ad infinitum.* Simply perusing what is readily available through the Internet will help anyone to note the interlocking relationships existing among organizations, powerfully situated individuals, and government.

A good place to start is a search on the Internet for the Atlantic Union. There is currently no such organization by that name, but you will find several websites that together provide an overview of this subversive cause. These websites will also show how many prominent men in America have been involved in a plan to merge the United States with Europe. You will be shocked to read some of the names of the individuals and organizations that have endorsed and even labored for such a development. Evidence showing this disloyalty comes from the individuals and organizations themselves, not just accusations from detractors.

A trade agreement between the United States and Europe, something endorsed by all the pro Atlantic Union individuals and organizations, would be one of the most important incremental steps on the way to even larger such unions, and then, ultimately, to a UN world government. Recall that the EU subordinates itself in its constitution to the UN.

One revealing place to have high on the list of any search is the Atlantic Council (AC). Formed in 1961, the goal it sought to accomplish half a century ago is what the proposed TTIP is designed to bring about today: immersion of the United States into a union with Europe. A 1975 policy statement issued by the AC while the future President George H. W. Bush served on its board of directors stated its desire to form institutions able to "deal adequately with problems with which no existing nation-state can cope successfully alone." An

AC publication entitled *The Future of the United Nations* praised "global interdependence" and added: "the UN system can and should perform the bulk of the global functions."

In addition to George H. W. Bush, the AC's Board of Directors during this period included such prominent government officials as Henry Kissinger (Secretary of State), Paul Nitze (Secretary of the Navy), William J. Casey (CIA Director), Brent Scowcroft (National Security Advisor), Eugene Rostow (Undersecretary of State), and Winston Lord (Assistant Secretary of State). All of these men and more of their fellow supporters of the AC held membership in the Council on Foreign Relations. Their backing of AC's goal indicates that many prominent men in America have an agenda to merge the United States with Europe as a step toward United Nations domination of mankind in a "new world order." And there are plenty more who have similar subversive credentials.

The AC states on its own website the need "to strengthen ... economic integration between Europe and the United States." This organization partners with NATO and the Atlantic Treaty Association.

Finally, until he was named secretary of defense during Obama's second term, then-Senator Charles Hagel was the chairman of the Atlantic Council. Imagine placing a man in charge of the defense of the United States who obviously wants to dissolve the United States by sending our country into a multinational organization linking the EU with North America. No enemy needs to invade — the men in charge of America will destroy the independence of our country without a shot being fired, unless the American people become aware of what is going on.

Under any sane definition it would be called treason.

As historian Arnold Toynbee once noted, "Civilizations die as a result of suicide, not murder."

The Transatlantic Policy Network (TPN) is a good example of an organization that straddles the Atlantic involving important members of the EU and America. The co-chair for a long time was U.S. Senator Robert Bennett (R-Utah). The goal of the TPN is to merge the EU and the United States by the year 2015. This corresponds to the timetable of the TTIP. Former Senator Bennett is also a good example of how a politician can stand for certain social mores, gaining the support of the pro-life movement for example, but work for an objective that will ultimately remove any say over our social issues by the American people. Positions of the EU concerning abortion, euthanasia, homosexuality, etc., have demonstrated that the level of morality and social mores differs greatly from the average American.

As of this writing, the TPN has five members of the Senate working with them, four of whom are Republicans. The 32 U.S. Representatives in the TPN are divided almost in half by party but include the Speaker of the House John Boehner. Most of these Republican Congressmen are not known to be members of the Social Democrats, yet are working for the same goal.

The members of Congress have taken an oath to uphold and defend the Constitution from all enemies, foreign and domestic, yet some are working with an organization that will ultimately do away with the Constitution.

Abraham Lincoln had a few thoughts about the only way we could lose our country. In an "Address Before the Young Men's Lyceum" of Springfield, Illinois, on January 27, 1838, he said:

> Shall we expect some transatlantic military giant, to step the Ocean, and crush us at a blow? Never! — All the armies of Europe, Asia and Africa combined with all the treasure of the earth (our own excepted) in their military chest; with a Bonaparte for a commander, could not by force, take a drink from the Ohio, or make a

track on the Blue Ridge, in a trial of a thousand years.... [I]f it ever reach us, it must spring up amongst us.

While perusing the Internet, we again suggest that you keep in mind that, in order to merge with Europe or any other country or group of countries, the United States would have to cancel the Declaration of Independence and ignore the U.S. Constitution. The evidence when looking at the organizations and individuals behind the promotion of modern trade agreements more than indicates this is their goal. It doesn't matter what their motives are; the consequences are clear: the end of the United States as we know it and the building of the New World Order.

While backers of the TTIP seek to tie our country to Europe, the similar Trans-Pacific Partnership (TPP) aims toward the identical sovereignty-destroying goal through a "free trade" agreement with Pacific Rim countries (Australia, Brunei, Canada, Chile, Japan, Malaysia, Mexico, New Zealand, Peru, Singapore, Vietnam, and the United States, and the possible inclusion of China as well). While no Pacific counterpart of the EU currently exists, plans for the TPP amount to a beginning step toward creation of such a government structure.

Economic integration is always a precursor to political integration — which is shown by the economic ties forged in Europe that have led to the political entity. the European Union. The TPP in the Pacific is what NAFTA was to America, a first major step. It could rightly be called a Pacific NAFTA.

Summarizing, concerning Europe, the TTIP process aims at uniting Europe and our nation. Concerning the Pacific, the TPP is in its embryonic stage and is no less a threat to American liberty.

Promoters of involving the United States in a TPP claim that it will stand up to the growing might of China in the Pacific. But what if, after we are locked in, the majority of other TPP nations agree to take in China? Most of the countries already involved in the negotiations for TPP have heavy Chinese investments in their country and have been growing very friendly with China.

7
Homeland Security

Russia

A disturbing development in foreign policy leading to entanglements is the growth of security arrangements between American national security agencies, our armed forces and their Russian counterparts.

It has grown to the extent that the head of Russia, Vladimir Putin, has mentioned America being Russia's "partner" more than once. President George W. Bush used this term as well. You can use the Internet to search for and confirm these statements.

It all began with the Open Skies Treaty allowing Russian aircraft to fly over our military bases within the United States, ostensibly to maintain the peace by spying on U.S. military preparedness.

A citizen of the United States is not allowed to fly over our military bases. These are no-fly zones that are well known to civilian pilots. Should this happen, the plane would be forced to land and the pilot interrogated, and a large fine and/or prison time could result. These no-fly zones were established to protect our military secrets as well as not to interfere in military aerial maneuvers. Now we keep secrets from our citizens but not a potential enemy.

Similarly, an accord was signed by Obama and Russian President Dmitry Medvedev allowing U.S. cargo planes to fly over Russia to supply U.S. troops in Afghanistan. This includes landing in Russian territory for refueling and other issues.

The net result has not only been closer ties between U.S. and Russian military and security personnel, it has also led to two alarming developments. First, Russian military aircraft have assumed a more aggressive attitude testing American early warning systems in Northern California, Guam, Alaska, and over carrier task forces in the Pacific, and also have provoked other nations such as Sweden by testing their military response to fly-overs of their territory.[8]

The partnership between American and Russian security forces led to an agreement in 2013 between FEMA and Russia for Russia to supply security personnel and their expertise at crowd control and security at

---

8. This author was on a flight from Seattle over the northern polar region to Schiphol Airport in the Netherlands. Russian MIG fighter aircraft attempted to use the radar image of the commercial airliner to penetrate American early warning defenses as an exercise over Iceland. They did not succeed, as we witnessed the Russian planes being chased off by American fighters.

major events in the United States. The Russians will more than likely not man any visible entrances or checkpoints, at least not at first, but will be on hand to lend advice and gain knowledge as to our security procedures. The immediate problem is that the Russians will be supplied with American equipment, and will learn how American security forces use this equipment and what the operating procedures are during emergencies.

This is an example of similar cooperative operations, such as an initiative that includes Russian Spetsnaz special forces units training with American Special Forces on American soil at Ft. Carson, Colorado.

In this way, the Russians find out about our procedures, the use of our equipment, and the capabilities of the American units. Needless to say, this information is vital to the operations in combat in any future war, but all done in the name of peace and combating terrorism.

If a private American citizen had supplied the same information to a Russian spy ring, he would have been prosecuted. In this case, it is our own government and high-level military officers supplying the Russians with military secrets, both on the ground and in the air.

The joint training exercise of NORAD and the Russian Federation Air Force, called Vigilant Eagle, allowed generals of the Russian Air Force to witness top secret facilities, equipment, and procedures at our Colorado-based NORAD command center. The American counterpart of the Russians, Brig. Gen. Richard Scobee, deputy director of operations at NORAD, said,

> [On] my first visit to Moscow I found out immediately that our cultures are very similar. More than any place I've been in the world, we value life.

It is disappointing to witness that men put in charge of our defense do not know history about the fact that the Soviet regime killed a minimum of 40 million of its own people. The Russian government is now led by those who participated in this carnage, such as ex-KGB officer Putin.

There is a great deal of evidence that much of the terrorism around the world that is blamed on Islam is in fact fueled by Russia. It certainly is armed by Russia with Russian and/or Chinese equipment. The evidence for this is not the subject for this book, but *if the reader takes the time* to research it, there is ample evidence on the Internet.

If this is the case, ask yourself the question: If I were a Russian officer, would it be helpful to understand how American security forces operate? Would I like to know how their equipment works, with the possibility of circumventing its use?

With the ability to overfly our bases, test our early warning capabilities, work with our Special Forces and internal security personnel, and actually be part of NORAD exercises, the Russians have a clear picture of our security and defense mechanisms — civil and military.

Lest the reader believe that we live in an era of the death of communism, go online and search out the May Day and Lenin's birthday celebrations in Red Square in Moscow each year. The Russian government does not allow demonstrations that they do not sanction. These demonstrations feature pictures of Lenin, Stalin, and a host of communist leaders. Aeroflot, the Russian airline, still uses the old hammer and sickle emblem, which is also displayed on the façade of the building housing the Russian foreign ministry in Moscow.

Under the Posse Comitatus Act, it is illegal to deploy U.S. military personnel inside of the United States to control civilians. Yet, the Obama administration signed an agreement to allow Mexican and Canadian troops into the U.S. during a state of emergency. The Russian agreement regarding security personnel appears to allow an even more dangerous precedent of allowing Russians to "assist" in crowd control and security.

One agreement begets another, until the Bill of Rights and the Constitution come under serious threat. One of the problems is that too many of our top military and intelligence community leaders are members of the Council on Foreign Relations. It is indeed rare when the Joint Chiefs of Staff does not have one, two, or more CFR members on its roster.

What we have outlined here is just the tip of the iceberg when it comes to U.S.-Russian partnership. An online search will reveal formal charters, FBI-FSB agreements, etc., that strengthen the partnership. Most of the entanglements have been signed by U.S.-Russian counterparts but not ratified by Congress.[9]

China

The imbalance of imports from China vs. exports to China has set the stage for China to use this imbalance against us as if we are already engaged in a war. And, to tell the truth, we already are; the American people do not yet know it. The war is just as real as if there were battles on land and sea, with casualty lists posted every day. The casualty lists in this case are factories and jobs

9. One such document is "A Charter for American-Russian Partnership and Friendship" signed by George H. W. Bush and released by the White House Press Secretary on June 17, 1992.

as a prelude to setting the stage for neutralizing the effectiveness of the American people to maintain their independence.

The Chinese People's Liberation Army declares each year that its primary enemy is the United States. Its leaders have even developed a video game featuring a conflict between their troops and U.S. troops to help train their personnel. This video game is similar to the violent games that American children play, except that in this one, the enemy is the U.S. Armed Forces.

The economic pundits are keeping our eyes on the least of the negatives involved and not the strategic moves China is making with the monies that flow out of our country into the Chinese communists' coffers. It is true that China owns a lot of our debt, but it is also true they are swimming in dollars as a result of their exportation of goods to America.

Here's what's happening: The Chinese are using these dollars to buy up the rest of the world. Now as we go through a litany of examples, please keep in mind that we are not opposed to Chinese; we are opposed to Chinese communist influence.

Nouveaux riches have grown up in the new Chinese economy, just as happened in Russia; however, it did not take long for the real Russian elite, the so-called ex-

KGB, to eliminate many of these "entrepreneurs" from the scene and simply confiscate their wealth and holdings. Totalitarians have had a nasty habit of doing this throughout history.

We believe that at some time in the future the same will happen in China. It is, after all, a communist empire. Russia tried to hide this for some years. The Chinese have not, only making it appear as if they are more liberal commercially.

When we refer to Chinese influence, it will all come back ultimately to building communism, not free enterprise. Just because the newly rich in China are well off doesn't make them anti-communist or pro-American or even make them trust us. Regardless, there has been a centuries-old distrust of Occidentals, and this has been reinforced by what the British and the American governments did to China from the 1800s up until 1949. You might say that we helped them in World War II, but a more correct way of putting it is that we set the stage for a communist government under Mao Zedong after the war — this story requires another book.

In the end, the newly rich Chinese will do what they are told. They have family in China that can be used as leverage should they get too uppity. Never underestimate the mind of a totalitarian when it comes to what they can use for leverage and how they will stop at nothing to gain their objectives. After all, the Russians have not only been stripping the newly wealthy in Russia of their holdings; they have been sending many of them off to prison in the process. The Chinese Communists have never been shy about imprisoning anyone who has the potential of opposing the communist state.

On the surface, many of the commercial deals being made outside of China will be made to look as if they are only business deals with the nouveaux riches. Most of the buying, however, comes from state-operated companies.[10]

In Iraq and Afghanistan, the Chinese are buying up mineral wealth, such as oil, iron ore, copper ore, etc. In some cases, American fighting men are guarding the roads in and out of the mines from the Taliban so that the Chinese can get their ore out to ship it to their smelters.

Likewise, the oil fields in Iraq are increasingly being operated by Chinese and the crude oil is going into Chinese hands.

10. In 2013, it was announced that a Chinese firm was buying the largest pork-processing firm in the world, Smithfield Foods of Virginia. All announcements pertaining to this deal mentioned that the Chinese firm was a private corporation, as did all English-language websites posted about this purchase. However, the Mandarin Chinese websites told a different story, and upon translation exposed the fact that the "private firm" was actually a Communist Party entity.

We have sent our men and women into harm's way in Iraq and Afghanistan, and in the end the Chinese reap the material benefits.

Throughout Latin America, China is loaning money to the governments and investing in mineral wealth there as well. It is no coincidence that the nations of Latin America are voting in communist leaders one after the other. As you look at the pattern, China is surrounding the United States by its activities in the southern half of the Western Hemisphere. Of course, Russia is part of this process as well, selling weapons to Latin American countries.

China has a significant presence at the new super port in Mexico, Lazero Cardenas. The port is being expanded in anticipation of ultimately building a super highway system rolling into the southern United States. Part of this initiative is the move to allow Mexican trucks to operate on American highways. Incidentally, the port of Lazero Cardenas was named after a Mexican president who was awarded the Stalin Peace Prize, later renamed the Lenin Peace Prize.

Chinese firms effectively run the Panama Canal. This is apparently not enough. A new enterprise of $40 billion to build a new shipping canal through communist Nicaragua has recently been announced by a

Chinese firm.

Contemplate what these things mean in any future war with China, Russia, or any ally of China.

In fact, if you look at the nations involved in the negotiations for the TPP, China has invested a great deal of money in them. These countries will be hard-pressed not to listen to China relative to their foreign policy. This influence will have sway on the votes by these countries on various boards, commissions, and courts within the TPP.

How does one form a partnership with a socialist country like China without losing some of our free-enterprise economy? It can't be done without seriously undermining the free-enterprise system and the freedom of the non-socialist partner. In addition, they use the U.S. dollars from selling us cheap goods to come back into our country to buy real property, thereby having increased influence on local, state, and ultimately the federal governments. Finally, many aspects of the so-called trade agreements place international controls on sectors that have no relationship to trade. All these things have an effect on our social, economic, and governmental systems.

There have been ongoing negotiations with the Chinese government to open up the investment market between the United States and China. There is a very important aspect of this investment that must always be considered: the American investments will be private and will have only a single focus — that of the owner's or owners' profit — whereas the Chinese investments will be influenced by the Chinese Communist government, one way or the other. Chinese investment will be part of a strategic government plan, not simply investment opportunities for individuals or nongovernment corporations.

While Chinese investment in the United States is in the low billions of dollars per year, the Chinese government is considering restructuring their foreign exchange reserves into real property in the United States. These reserves amount to 3.4 trillion dollars. At first, such an investment would seem to be a boon. However, after the investment comes local influence on our economy and local government.

Just as *Agenda 21* has an influence on local government with a coordinated international plan (see the next chapter), likewise any Chinese investments would have the coordinated effect of the Chinese government toward a common political goal, unlike American investments that would simply be driven by profit for the individual company.

The idea of opening up our country to Chinese investments is supported by the leadership of such organizations as the Carnegie Endowment for International Peace, another group posing as one thing but involved for years in promoting international merger and dominated by leadership from the Council on Foreign Relations. Alger Hiss was president of the Endowment from 1946 to 1949. In addition, he was a CFR member — as well as a Soviet spy.

It is interesting that while our government is moving forward to allow more and more Chinese investment in the U.S., the same people who promote the TPP/TTIP are using the menace of a Chinese economic threat to win over adherents to these so-called trade agreements.

An article in the CFR organ *Foreign Affairs* online, "For Transatlantic Trade, This Time Is Different," posted on February 26, 2013, provided a "Snapshot" summary of the negotiations for the TTIP agreement:

> In the past, U.S. and European negotiators have tried and failed to create a unified transatlantic market. But the trade talks that President Obama announced this month have a much better chance of succeeding, thanks to a greater

need for economic growth on both sides, *the threat of China's illiberal economic behavior*, and the desire to give U.S.-European relations a new purpose. [Emphasis added.]

It seems that whether China is a threat or a friend depends on what agreement the CFR membership is trying to convince people to support at any given time.

Foreign entanglements with socialist countries are not in the interest of the American people.

8
Agenda 21

I n 1992, Rio de Janeiro welcomed 35,000 government officials, journalists, environmental activists, and others to the United Nations Conference on Environment and Development, more widely known as the "Earth Summit."

Among the many documents emanating from this huge gathering was the 1,100-page *Agenda 21*. It contains plans to bring the world under total control of the United Nations during the 21st century (thus the number 21 in its title).

The route laid out in this comprehensive plan calls in part for local governments to submit to rules and regulations addressing various environmental matters. The massive document urges a transferring of virtually all aspects of freedom and legal independence to the world body in the name of protecting the environment. The document's foreword approvingly states:

- "*Agenda 21* proposes an array of actions which are intended to be implemented by every person on earth...."

- "[It] will require a reorientation of all human society unlike anything the world has ever experienced...."

- "There are specific actions which are intended to be taken ... by every person on earth."

The Rio accord, covering all aspects of the conference, including *Agenda 21*, won the signature of President George H. W. Bush — who attended the event. It wasn't submitted to the Senate for ratification because it was never intended to be a treaty ratified by nations. In a WorldNetDaily article posted on February 3, 2012, Henry Lamb explained:

> Nothing in *Agenda 21* is legally binding on any government until a government — at any level — adopts an *Agenda 21* recommendation as a law or ordinance, or as an executive order such as EO 12852 [creating the President's Council on Sustainable Development] issued by President Bill Clinton in 1993 in response to *Agenda 21* recommendation 8.7.

Therefore, its partisans work with various levels of government to implement *Agenda 21* through presidential executive orders, federal and state environmental regulations, state "comprehensive planning" laws and regulations, and a stealth program that lures many local and county supervisory boards and planning commissions into incorporating *Agenda 21* recommendations without knowing that they originated with the United Nations, or even *Agenda 21* for that matter. The end result: a UN presence that will lead to UN domination.

Agenda 21's movement toward its intended goal is being accomplished by local governments who become members of the International Council for Local Environmental Initiatives (ICLEI), a "nongovernmental organization" (NGO) formally associated with the United Nations. Its original name says it all: an *international* council that is aimed at *local* implementation of environmental regulations. It is especially revealing that ICLEI now prefers to be known as "ICLEI — Local Governments for Sustainability." Once unsuspecting local officials sign on to regulations frequently carrying the appealing name "sustainability," the UN's foot is in the door. But rarely has anyone at the local level known that the UN is behind what they have accepted.

ICLEI enlists local governments, city councils, county commissioners, etc., to voluntarily adopt UN initiatives and mandates, almost always without the people or their local officials having any awareness that they are ceding significant power to the UN. The new relationship is frequently entered into by local government officials who rarely, if ever, fully understand what is involved. In fact, many mayors and commissioners have been surprised to learn that their governmental body had agreed to ties to the UN through ICLEI. However, *literally hundreds of American communities belong to ICLEI.*

In many towns, cities, and counties across America (and elsewhere throughout the globe), environmental rules are being imposed from the top down through international agreements. At the same time, newly adopted programs receive support from the bottom up from members of activist groups who support the UN and/or accept the widely circulated environmental scares. Rarely do any of the local officials know that the UN is the behind-the-scenes sponsor of these programs. The tactic has been referred to as pressure from above and pressure from below. It is a pincers movement aimed at the American people, their businesses, their property rights, and even their nation.

Many have recently been awakened to this danger. Local government is closest to the people and customarily wins their respect, but not if an international body moves in to impose its international decrees. Implementation of *Agenda 21* mandates through ICLEI or some other UN front group disconnects the people from their own local government.

Only a short time ago, anyone could find ICLEI on the Internet and, in two easily accomplished additional steps, learn its UN connection. Two clicks on the ICLEI site would take anyone to *Agenda 21*, and then to the UN. There could be no question about this revealing relationship. But information disseminated by The John Birch Society caused such a stir that the ICLEI website was remarkably altered, and the direct link to the UN disappeared. Thus, materials urging everyone to see for themselves the UN's relationship to *Agenda 21* and ICLEI became obsolete. This was only the first step to obfuscate what was going on with this initiative.

However, the ICLEI-UN connection can still be found through diligent searching of the two websites. The removal of the easily shown proof of this relationship leads to two conclusions: 1) Opposition to this scheme has been effective, and 2) reliance on secrecy to implement it indicates treachery because government at any level should always be an "open book."

More than bringing local areas into compliance with environmental demands, *Agenda 21* is a plan to bring all local government and all property under UN control without the citizens of any area realizing what is going on until it is too late.

In some areas of the United States, regulations gov-

erning the property rights of local citizens were beginning to stifle economic development before the citizens
found out the source of the problem.

Many communities have withdrawn from ICLEI,
but for a time were still listed on the ICLEI site as being
members. By not taking their names off the list, ICLEI
hid just how many local governing agencies canceled
membership or were no longer paying dues. In addition,
there were fewer communities signing on. As of this
writing, the ratio of those leaving to those joining is two-
to-one and climbing. This is the result of citizen activism
informing local opinion molders and voters.

The efforts of local citizens in finding out their communities were members of ICLEI, then influencing their
local governments to withdraw membership, became
such a problem for ICLEI that they ceased listing which
communities were members in the U.S. on their website.
This was obviously done in an attempt to shut down
citizen activism in communities holding ICLEI membership. So much for transparency! Anyone may access the
list of members in any country around the world except
for America, since only in our country are our citizens
able to organize against ICLEI successfully.

A great deal more can be learned about *Agenda 21*

at JBS.org and *The New American*.

Again, the ultimate goal of *Agenda 21*, the United Nations, and many other initiatives is international control of everyone and everything. Many who work to achieve it refer to it as the New World Order.

9
The New World Order

All of what we have discussed so far leads to an international order. Those who are working to impose it on mankind refer to their goal as the "New World Order" (NWO). These are their words, not a label imposed on them by a conservative adversary.

Keep in mind the adage of Lord Acton that power tends to corrupt and apply that to a world government so removed from the people that inevitably any idea of liberty would be exhausted by the power of the state. Couple this with the fact that it would mean an alliance with socialist/communist states. Then top it off by noting that CFR-types in the United States advocate a NWO, and any thought of a benevolent world government would be a fantasy.

The first documented use of the term "New World Order" by Karl Marx and Frederick Engels appeared in their *The Holy Family* written in February 1845. With emphasis in the original, it stated:

> The revolutionary movement which began in 1789 in the Cercle Social...gave rise to the communist idea ... of the *new world order*.

The term had been used previously by other internationalists, but here we see it identified as "the communist idea." What Marx and Engels wrote in this instance was criticism of others who sought to lead the street-level communist movement. They wanted to be its sole leaders and would never allow dissent.

Over many decades, and increasingly into the latter part of the 20th century, noted internationalists and open communists have made reference to a need for the "new world order." The list includes socialist author H.G. Wells, Mikhail Gorbachev, Fidel Castro, Henry Kissinger, David Rockefeller, Joseph R. Biden, Jr., and even the Chinese Communist newspaper *China Daily*. It also includes President George H. W. Bush, who repeatedly stated that the goal of the first war against Iraq was a New World Order.

On September 11, 1990, when announcing that he would use authorization supplied by the United Nations to commit U.S. forces as the response to Iraq's invasion of Kuwait, Bush stated:

> Out of these troubled times, our fifth objective
> — a new world order — can emerge. We are now
> in sight of a United Nations that performs as

envisioned by its founders.[11]

In August 1991, Mr. Bush made the creation of a New World Order, by that name, an *official policy* of the government of the United States. The State Department issued his proclamation in a document entitled *National Security Strategy of the United States.* The preface, titled "A NEW WORLD ORDER," is signed by George H. W. Bush; this is a completely unconstitutional act.

Authorization for the 1991 war against Iraq was supplied by the United Nations. Beginning in 2003, the identical process called for by a UN Security Council resolution was employed to send U.S. forces into Iraq again. Clearly, these wars amounted to subjugation and use of our armed forces by the United Nations, but were made to appear as an American initiative. In each instance, the requirement for a congressional declaration of war as clearly spelled out by the Constitution's Article I, Section 8 was ignored — and Congress allowed it to happen under the aegis of the United Nations.

George W. Bush's later support for the Free Trade Area of the Americas, as well as the Security and Prosperity Partnership and North American Union, was

11. This can be verified by accessing the Internet's YouTube. Search for George H. W. Bush and the New World Order. In several additional postings of statements made by the then-president before Congress and in televised speeches, he repeatedly linked mention of the New World Order to the United Nations.

simply an extension of the official policy for a New World Order enunciated by his father. But the second President Bush sought to bring it about in the name of trade as well as war.

Regardless of their motivation, a number of prominent people around the globe in cooperation with members of the government of the United States are working to establish a one-world government. Numerous international agreements made since World War II have been incrementally leading toward that goal.

The United Nations

Along with the agreements that are undermining the independence of various countries, there are agreements and institutions working to merge banking institutions and even change nations' paper currencies. The establishment of the World Bank and the International Monetary Fund (IMF), both related to the United Nations and both heavily funded by U.S. taxpayers, has placed great financial power into the hands of the United Nations. Abandonment of their currencies by numerous European states followed creation of the euro and the EU's bank.

The international and domestic policies of our own government have led to the use of taxpayers' money to help international corporations, prop up foreign governments, and even replace some governments. They have also enticed national leaders to sign agreements that result in more and more international regulation and control administered by the World Bank and the IMF.

To illustrate the fundamental differences between our system and that of the rest of the world, and especially the United Nations, one needs to take a closer look at the UN's attitude about fundamental rights possessed by every person on earth.

One of the most revealing of various UN documents that provide the thinking and ultimate goals of the UN is its 1948 *Universal Declaration of Human Rights*. Nowhere in this document appears the fact that our rights come from a Creator — God — as is clearly stated in the U.S. Declaration of Independence.

The UN *Declaration* lists a great many rights that all people possess, even more than appear in U.S. Bill of Rights. But there are a number of welfare programs presented as rights as well. Very few have read this UN *Declaration* closely and are, therefore, unaware of the significance of its Article 29, which states: "These rights and freedoms may in no case be exercised contrary to the purposes and principles of the United Nations."

In other words, everyone can enjoy freedom of speech as long as you are not speaking against the UN's purposes and principles. You can have the right of assembly, as long as your gathering does not oppose UN purposes and actions. You have the right to exercise your religion unless what you believe counters UN mandates and policies, such as preventing abortion or refusing to embrace homosexuality. And so on! Under the UN's attitude toward rights, there are essentially no rights other than what the UN tolerates.

In 1966, the UN issued another telling example of its thinking entitled the *International Covenant on Civil and Political Rights*. This *Covenant* was designed to read like the Bill of Rights of the U.S. Constitution, but there are major differences.

Article 14 of the *Covenant* states that "everyone shall be entitled to a fair and public hearing." That appears to parallel the guarantee in the Bill of Rights "to a speedy and public trial." But, the *Covenant* then declares: "The press and public may be excluded from all or part of a trial for reasons of morals, public order." This grants legitimacy for secret trials, a hallmark of despotisms throughout history.

To further make the point that there are major differences between the United Nations attitude toward rights and the Bill of Rights, we include two more examples. The First Amendment of the U.S. Bill of

Rights declares without qualification, "Congress shall make no law respecting the establishment of religion, or prohibiting the free exercise thereof; or abridging the freedom of speech or of the press...." Repeat: Congress "shall make no law"! By way of contrast, Article 18 of the *Covenant* states, "Everyone shall have the right to freedom of thought, conscience and religion," but it then asserts that "Freedom to manifest one's religion or beliefs may be subject only to such limitations as are prescribed by law and are necessary."

Likewise, Article 21 of the *Covenant* purports to guarantee the right of peaceful assembly, but it then permits the state to limit this right for "national security or public safety, public order [or] the protection of public health or morals." What dictator couldn't use that qualification to prevent peaceful assembly?

Our Bill of Rights says no law may be passed to cancel fundamental rights. Both the *Universal Declaration* and the *Covenant* say the UN can enact laws to control or trample on such rights.

Yet our Senate ratified the *Covenant*, even though only a small portion of the Senate was present. This ratification was accomplished without fanfare or opposition, yet the *Covenant* was given a high place alongside our own system.

A telling omission from the UN's listing of "rights" enjoyed by the people is the right to keep and bear arms. It is never mentioned. Quite the opposite; the UN is attempting to have every country disarm its citizens and leave weapons only in the hands of a UN Security Force, supposedly to enforce the peace. But as history has revealed, peace according to the UN is the absence of opposition to its rule.

The United Nations Arms Trade Treaty is a case in point. The UN wants to regulate all trade in firearms. Its provisions are intended to apply not just to "arms dealers." It would effectively place possession of all guns under UN monitoring and control, including sales between private parties, and even within families whose members may swap firearms.

Consideration of the UN Arms Trade Treaty caused such a stir among American gun-rights and Second Amendment partisans that the treaty wasn't submitted to the Senate for ratification. However, the Obama administration signed the treaty on September 25, 2013, and will presumably submit it to the Senate for ratification in the future in spite of the lack of support for the treaty in Congress and among the American people.

In other words, Congress and the American people said one thing; the administration leaders another.

There is an agenda by key American leaders to subjugate our system and place it under UN control. The gun issue is a visible part of that agenda.

Anyone passing by the UN headquarters building in New York will see a prominent statue of a handgun with its barrel tied into a knot. It sends a message that the UN has a goal of eliminating handguns — unless in the hands of the authorities, the same condition that existed in Nazi Germany, the USSR, and other modern totalitarian regimes. Dictators cannot tolerate their citizenry having the ability to defend themselves.

A test vote, of sorts, was taken in the U.S. Senate on March 23, 2013 on an amendment to "uphold Second Amendment rights and prevent the United States from entering into the United Nations Arms Trade Treaty." While the amendment was adopted by a vote of 53 to 46, this means that 46 senators voted against this amendment that supported the Second Amendment of the Bill of Rights.

As for treaties entered into by the United States, we stated earlier that many of these treaties declare right up front that they are subsidiary regional agreements under the auspices of the UN, that they conform to the principles and purposes of the UN, and/or that they are made in agreement with the UN Security Council or General Assembly.

America's leaders have been slowly subjecting our nation's foreign and domestic policies to the United Nations through treaties and agreements without the American people realizing what is happening.

Strict constitutionalists have been warning for some time that Congress has been approving mandates "recommended" by the UN which are detrimental to our country. The mass media have ignored these warnings, with the result that very few Americans are aware of the potential danger or its source. And most opponents of the UN and their arguments are never mentioned in the mass media.

The agreements and treaties the United States has entered into with the various divisions of the United Nations span the entire gamut of man's life and activity. The list that follows first mentions the general area of concern (in italics), followed by the UN's activity in that area:

- *Fundamental Rights*: Universal Declaration of Human Rights, International Covenant on Civil and Political Rights

- *Banking, Economics, and Monetary Policy*: International Monetary Fund, World Bank, United Nations Economic and Social Council

- *Trade*: World Trade Organization

- *Industry*: United Nations Industrial Development Organization

- *Education*: United Nations Children's Fund, the United Nations Educational, Scientific and Cultural Organization

- *Women*: United Nations Entity for Gender Equality and the Empowerment of Women

- *Birth Control, Abortion, Population Control*: United Nations Population Fund

- *Private Ownership of Firearms*: United Nations Arms Trade Treaty (heavy UN regulation of privately owned firearms — not yet ratified by Congress. Obama supported ratification but ran into heated opposition in Congress.)

- *Oceans and Their Tributaries*: United Nations Convention on the Law of the Sea, International Seabed Authority, and International Maritime Organization (Ocean tributaries means the rivers that flow out of all countries and their tributaries within the interior of the countries.)

- *Courts That Can Supersede American Courts*: International Court of Justice, International Criminal Court

- *Labor*: International Labor Organization

- *Agriculture*: Food and Agriculture Organization, International Fund for Agriculture Development, and World Food Programme

- *Environment*: United Nations Environment Programme and Global Environment Facility

- *Tourism*: United Nations World Tourism Organization

Except for private ownership of firearms and some provisions concerning the oceans, the United States Senate has already acceded to the above UN entities and, in the process, has subordinated the United States to the UN. Executive orders have frequently been issued by a president of the United States to implement agreements, at least in part, when ratification by the Senate hasn't been achieved.

There is much more. But we hope our point has been made. Space limitations dictate that we don't list all of these real and potential threats to the freedom of individuals and nations.

Keep in mind that these are only the direct entities of the United Nations. The list does not include entanglements entered into via UN subsidiary organizations such as NAFTA, NATO, etc.

10
Treaties Supersede the Constitution?

One of the more incorrect beliefs regarding international agreements is the contention that, once ratified by the U.S. Senate, a treaty supersedes the U.S. Constitution. This is an attitude that has been implanted into the minds of the American people by some who are determined to deliver America into the New World Order. But treaties do not supersede the Constitution. America's founders were very clear about this.

> I say the same as to the opinion of those who consider the grant of the treaty-making power as boundless. If it is, then we have no Constitution.

> — Thomas Jefferson, September 1803

The main obstacle to the New World Order envisioned by the one-world planners has been, and remains, the Constitution of the United States of America. Unique in both its foundational principles and structure, the constitutional system established by America's Founding Fathers — abused though it may be by decades of sustained assault on the one hand and neglect on the other

— continues to stymie the architects of global government. Hence, globalists have spread the claim that treaties override the Constitution as a way to circumvent the venerable document.

The House of Representatives has no vote regarding treaties, and that in itself is an indication that treaties cannot supersede the Constitution, since both Houses must pass any amendment or law. It makes no sense to say, therefore, that a treaty is a law superior to the Constitution if the House of Representatives is left out of the picture. Some agreements, especially trade agreements, are approved by both Houses of Congress. Most people don't understand the reason for this, including most members of Congress. But both Houses are included because the Constitution mandates that Congress — the whole Congress, not just the Senate — regulates commerce with foreign nations.

Therefore treaties involving trade actually would be overriding the portion of the Constitution requiring that Congress shall regulate commerce. Delegation of its authority by Congress is barred by the Constitution, yet modern trade agreements transfer this power to an international body. If at some time in the future public pressure were to be brought to bear on the government to stop and/or reject these trade pacts, since the

Constitution gives the exclusive power to regulate foreign trade to the entire Congress, then any treaty that regulates foreign trade would have to be rejected on the basis that the Constitution grants this power to the entire Congress, not just the Senate. Based on these considerations, the powers-that-be have required that both Houses approve trade "agreements" instead of having the Senate approve trade "treaties." The agreements created in this manner still carry the weight of treaties.

Trade agreements ceding Congress's constitutional authorization regarding commerce to an international body may not seem to be that serious until one remembers that Congress represents the people of the United States. Therefore, the people have lost some of their rights over their own economy to an international power, however large or small it may be.

Often overlooked is just how important the free enterprise system is to the well-being of Americans, both in quality of life and of liberty itself. To allow outside forces to acquire control over it is to endanger the future of the American people.

It is highly doubtful that the UN Charter would have been ratified by the U.S. Senate in 1945 without the inclusion of Article 2, Paragraph 7, which states:

> Nothing contained in the present Charter shall authorize the United Nations to intervene in matters which are essentially within the domestic jurisdiction of any state or shall require the Members to submit such matters to settlement under the present Charter.

These words and their meaning seem clear enough. However, what the UN provides with one hand, it takes away with the other. Article 2, Paragraph 7 of the Charter also states that "this principle shall not prejudice the application of enforcement measures under Chapter VII." While the first portion of Article 2, Paragraph 7 says one thing, the second part provides a loophole that allows such intervention. Over the years, this loophole has been employed over and over again as the UN regularly interferes in the internal affairs of nations, including the use of armed forces to enforce UN mandates and resolutions.

Regardless of the rightness or wrongness of the arguments that led to such action, the precedent has been set to use armed might to enforce UN edicts. Through trade agreements and UN treaties, covenants, conventions, and courts, total international control over the American economy could well become a reality.

The Dulles Attitude Contradicts the Founders

The claim that treaties supersede the Constitution was emphasized in 1952 by John Foster Dulles, who would soon be named Secretary of State in the Eisenhower administration. In a speech before a regional meeting of the American Bar Association (ABA) in Louisville, Kentucky, he asserted:

> Treaties make international law and they also make domestic law. Under our Constitution, treaties become the supreme law of the land.... Treaties, for example, can take powers away from the Congress and give them to the federal government or to some international body, and they can cut across the rights given to the people by the constitutional Bill of Rights.

It is hardly surprising that such an attitude would be offered by Dulles, who was one of the founders of the Council on Foreign Relations and a life-long closet internationalist. His assertion, however, amounts to a serious misinterpretation of the Constitution. Happily, we can turn to several of the Founders for their thoughts on what treaties can and cannot do.

James Madison, who was secretary of the 1787 Constitutional Convention, and has been justifiably called "the Father of the Constitution," said of the treaty power:

> I do not conceive that power is given to the President and the Senate to dismember the empire, or alienate any great, essential right. I do not think the whole legislative authority have this power. The exercise of the power must be consistent with the object of the delegation.

In his authoritative reference work, *A Manual of Parliamentary Practice*, Thomas Jefferson declared:

> Surely the President and Senate cannot do by treaty what the whole government is interdicted from doing in any way.

This is not only sound legal opinion; it is plain common sense. If the Bill of Rights and the whole Constitution were to have any lasting force and meaning, the men who authored such documents would never have intended that our nation's Constitution could be completely undone by means of a treaty, or series of treaties.

We have already quoted Jefferson's opinion on the matter. Let us now look at the thinking of Alexander Hamilton, who among the Founding Fathers was a political opponent of Jefferson. He maintained:

> A treaty cannot be made which alters the
> Constitution of the country or which infringes
> any express exceptions to the power of the
> Constitution of the United States.

On another occasion, Hamilton wrote:

> The only constitutional exception to the power of
> making treaties is that it shall not change the
> Constitution.... On natural principles, a treaty,
> which should manifestly betray or sacrifice pri-
> mary interests of the state, would be null.

Throughout our history, American jurists have stated that treaties do not alter or supersede the Constitution. In *New Orleans vs. United States* (1836), future Supreme Court Justice Joseph Story and Justice Stephen J. Field held that what the Constitution forbids cannot be altered by legislation or treaty. The opposite opinion, given by Dulles and adopted by others, is of recent origin and was never the intent of the Constitution or its framers.

It says a great deal about the legal profession, at least in Kentucky, if an ABA meeting there would allow Dulles to get away with saying that treaties could legally cut across the Bill of Rights.

Through the misuse of the treaty-making provision, the one-worlders have taken huge strides in their effort to turn the founders upside down. It is of paramount importance, therefore, that Americans exercise special vigilance concerning all treaties. Unfortunately, we find just the opposite to be the case. The American public today is totally oblivious to the use of treaties that are, in their reality, intended to sweep away our constitutional protections. The blame rests jointly on the nation's deficient education system that fails to teach constitutional principles, along with the mass media, which has kept important information and perspective from the public.

If the internationalists are correct and treaty law does supersede the Constitution, then we have already lost it and its Bill of Rights through acceptance of such documents as the UN's *Universal Declaration of Human Rights* and the *International Covenant on Civil and Political Rights*. Only a fool or an international socialist would say this is the case.

The UN General Assembly adopted the *International Covenant on Civil and Political Rights* in 1966. But it wasn't ratified by the U.S. Senate for many years. Even though it was backed by the Carter administration in 1979, other pressing domestic and international concerns prevented the Senate from considering ratification. It wasn't considered until the administration of George H. W. Bush, when, on April 2, 1992, a mere handful of Senators ratified the *Covenant*.

The handful employed a little-known aspect of the Constitution's grant of power to the Senate to ratify treaties. Article II, Section 2 states that the president "shall have power ... to make treaties, provided two thirds of the Senators *present* concur." (Emphasis added.) This allows a minuscule number of senators to act for the entire Senate and the nation itself. And this is what occurred on April 2, 1992.

On that date, the Senate had finished work on a completely separate matter and most senators had departed the Senate chamber. Senate Majority Leader George Mitchell (D-Maine), Senator Jay Rockefeller (D-W.Va.), and Senator Ted Stevens (R-Alaska) remained. With Rockefeller in the chair, Mitchell conducted a three-minute session beginning with his requests to the chair that consideration of the *International Covenant* be accomplished in executive session, that no amendments can be added, and that reconsideration of the matter be barred. Seated in the chair on this occasion, Rockefeller acquiesced. Letters supporting ratification from Senators Claiborne Pell (D-R.I.), Albert Gore (D-Tenn.), and

Daniel Moynihan (D-N.Y.) were then referenced and inserted into the *Congressional Record* for that date. Mitchell then noted that his action enjoyed "approval of the Republican leader" who, at that time, was Senator Robert Dole (R-Kan.).

Sitting in the chair, Rockefeller asked for a voice vote, changed his mind when he realized that the two Senators before him couldn't produce much audible assent for the TV coverage to note, and asked instead for the yeas to stand. He then looked around the empty chamber as though he were counting standees, and pronounced the measure passed. (A videotape of the proceedings by C-SPAN shows this charade.) Three senators "present" had ratified the UN's *Covenant*. In his statement supporting ratification, Senator Moynihan wrote that the provisions of the *Covenant* "will now become binding international obligations of the United States."

Does the UN's *International Covenant on Civil and Political Rights* (which allows the UN to cancel all of the rights it lists) supersede the Constitution's Bill of Rights? According to Senator Moynihan — with no objection from the others who accomplished this treachery — it would surely seem that it does. But only if the American people are fooled into thinking that treaties supersede the Constitution.

United Nations Compliance

Let us return to the threat that international agreements made today must be in compliance with the *Charter of the United Nations*. This includes any military agreements and pacts. Most Americans don't realize that NATO, for instance, is a UN subordinate, a fact confirmed by the NATO Treaty itself.

The "Preamble" of the NATO Treaty states that: "the Parties to this Treaty reaffirm their faith in the purposes and principles of the United Nations." Then in Article 1, the text of the treaty makes clear its subordination to the UN; and it does so again in Articles 5 and 7.

The sad fact is that, since World War II, the United States has not committed our armed forces to any combat situation that has not been under the auspices of the UN or one of its subsidiaries such as NATO. In case after case, our forces have been sent into war under the authority supplied by the United Nations: Korea, Vietnam, Lebanon, Somalia, Bosnia, Kosovo, Iraq, Afghanistan, etc. In some cases our troops have actually served with UN flags flying over them as in Korea, or with UN insignia prominently shown on their uniforms and equipment.

Seldom have these conflicts had permanent resolution. Instead, they have become endless states-of-war

(Korea) or seemingly endless no-win wars where the U.S. forces eventually capitulate. Our armed forces have been placed in various areas around the globe for decades. And, the continuing list of conflicts has, in turn, resulted in repeated crises, as in Korea. They have also generated increased hatred for the United States among citizens who don't like foreign troops stationed in their countries.

If the United Nations has this kind of control over our armed forces, what kind of control do you think it would have over our economy through trade agreements that come under its purview?

In treaty after treaty and agreement after agreement, when you wade through the mountain of paper and cross references to other treaties, it becomes clear that these pacts entangle America not so much with another nation but with a world body — the United Nations. The ties to the UN may be found in the opening paragraphs of a pact, as in some of the cases we have referred to. In others, they are buried deeply within the agreements. They show that the ultimate authority is, in fact, the UN.

It may even be necessary to look at two or three agreements, treaties, or covenants to learn how they link together before you reach the UN. NAFTA provides a good example of virtually hidden — but real — linkage when one discovers mention of the *United Nations*

Convention on the Recognition and Enforcement of Foreign Arbitral Awards as part of the settlement processes under NAFTA. You have to read that *Convention* before you get a full sense of NAFTA.

11
Nothing Happens in Politics Unless Someone Planned It That Way

Presdent Franklin Delano Roosevelt is purported to have claimed: "In politics, nothing happens by accident. If it happens, you can bet it was planned that way." Whether he actually said this has been questioned, but the quote appears frequently because it accurately points to motivations that spur what is happening to our country.

This being the case, then we say again that certain people or groups of people want what is happening.

Consider the fable entitled *Gulliver's Travels*, with Gulliver being the American people. Strings are being laid across the sleeping giant, who doesn't notice what is happening to him. When he awakens, there are many small strings that would not bind him singly, but when laid across him together render the giant powerless.

Had Gulliver awakened early as the strings were being put across his body, he would never have become a prisoner. The same can be said of the American people: If they wake up before too many strings are placed across them, they will remain free. If not, they will become powerless creatures in a New World Order.

Most students in America are taught that some form

of international order is desirable. They have never been told that the vast majority of nations operate under some form of socialism and/or government control. Other peoples are not as free as the citizens of the United States — or as well-to-do.

If America becomes bogged down in an international order, the majority of countries would simply vote away our citizens' wealth through confiscatory legislation and our freedoms through various entanglements. We are rapidly approaching that situation.

Should the path we are on continue to lead us in this direction, the Bill of Rights would be extinct. Freedom to speak, assemble, worship, etc., would be terminated. And, the Second Amendment would cease to exist. Remember that none of the UN's documents purporting to dispense and protect rights includes the right to keep and bear arms.

Agreements already in place or under consideration must comply with the UN Charter or with some relatively obscure UN commission, covenant, or program. UN documents claiming to guarantee freedom to people must comply with the principles of the United Nations. While they acknowledge the existence of rights, they then state that all rights can be abolished or altered so that the UN itself will be supreme. In short, freedoms granted by the UN can be cancelled by the UN. Further, whoever controls the majority of the votes in the UN General Assembly can establish other rules and goals for all of mankind. The United States has not fared well in that body. Most countries vote at least 70 percent of the time against the interests of the American people.

William F. Jasper, whose "outrageous" 1989 warning of a centralized European Union was not believed at the time, authored another telling article in the October 22, 2012 issue of *The New American*. In "United Nations: On the Brink of Becoming a World Government," he wrote:

> On October 14, 2009, Lord Christopher Monckton, former science advisor to British Prime Minister Margaret Thatcher, delivered a scathing refutation of the concept of human-caused global warming at Bethel University in St. Paul, Minnesota. During his presentation, Lord Monckton focused on the UN climate treaty that was being proposed for the United Nations Climate Change Conference in Copenhagen that December. He warned:
>
> > I read that treaty. And what it says is this: that a world government is going to be created. The word "government" actually

appears as the first of the three purposes of the new entity. The second purpose is the transfer of wealth from the countries of the West to third world countries.... And the third purpose of this new entity, this government, is enforcement.

Not just any government, mind you. "They are about to impose a communist world government on the world," warned Monckton.

The point is that the American people and our business community are being sold on agreements about trade, the environment, civilian disarmament, and other matters under false flags. These pacts pose enormous danger to the future of our country, our economic life, even life itself, whether William F. Jasper or Monckton are right or not.

Since the *Communist Manifesto* was written by Karl Marx and Frederick Engels in 1848, the goal of all communists and their socialist brethren has always been world government. They have never deviated from this goal. Their minions all over the world, including within the United States, have been working diligently to establish a New World Order. Of course, they want to establish it under a Marxian system.

The number of communist states is growing, hidden behind a false claim that "communism is dead." Former openly communist countries are now in the hands of individuals who are "ex-communists," some of them even "ex-terrorists." This is particularly true in the lands south of the U.S. border. From Nicaragua to Venezuela to Brazil to Argentina and back up again, leaders follow the communist/socialist pattern. Here again, search online for the Latin American rulers and the political parties backing them and you will find startling information that the mass media never mentions: a large majority of the Latin American countries are ruled by militant socialist parties and leaders.[12]

Our nation simply cannot afford to form alliances and agreements with people who are only posing as democrats and lovers of liberty but have something else in mind. The same holds true for entanglements with the European Union and with many of the Pacific Rim nations.

Don't be fooled into believing that proponents of world government are trying to establish something that will benefit mankind. The end result they seek will be bigger governments that are totally separated from the

12. The book *Disinformation*, by Lt. Gen. Ion Mihai Pacepa and Ronald J. Rychlak, WND Books, Washington, DC, 2013, goes even further in revealing the communist nature and control of several Latin American leaders. Gen. Pacepa defected to the West after serving as the head of the KGB's surrogate in Romania while it was under Russian control.

individual; governments in which the voter will have minimal influence, if any. And their goal will be a world government in which the United States will merely be one among many. As we write, there are 193 member nations in the UN. And the veto our nation possesses as a permanent member of the UN Security Council remains in the hands of U.S. leaders who, far from resisting the UN's stealthy progression toward total power, applaud this ominous development and pose no threat to it being finalized.

We have only begun to touch on the ramifications of foreign entanglements. We trust that you now begin to see how the agreements, treaties, pacts, etc., have the potential to change not only our American system of government, but our society as well. The danger to our way of living, our economy, and our liberty is huge. Generally, the American people are uninformed and misinformed about what is transpiring. It is not totally their fault, because they have been deprived of the information needed to make an informed opinion.

A massive educational effort must therefore be undertaken by those who do know and are determined enough to carry it out.

As we have stated, the U.S. Constitution is the largest stumbling block to a world government — that and the American people. If these two impediments are removed, the militant socialists will begin their hidden program reminiscent of the USSR and China in the early years of consolidating power and control. Hate is a main ingredient of organized socialism — hatred of capitalism, religion, and traditional society. The only thing that stands in the way of unleashing this hatred is an informed electorate among the American people.

We invite the reader to spend some time on the Internet researching whether what we have presented is believable. A good starting point is JBS.org. There you will find great detail covering the broad spectrum of what we have covered in these pages: North American Union, United Nations, *Agenda 21*, etc.

Once you become satisfied that what we have presented is correct, then you have arrived at a crossroads: Do you get involved in doing something about it, or go back to doing only what you did before — usually nothing? The most effective way to get involved is to become a part of a concerted education/action program already at work all over the country. It is The John Birch Society.

Please choose one of the following ways to start on the path of preserving freedom: go to JBS.org on the Internet; write us at P. O. Box 8040, Appleton, WI 54912; or call us at 1-800-JBS-USA1. You'll be glad you did — and so will the children of today and tomorrow.

The least anyone can do is inform their friends and family about what is going on — please perform this minimal task. The more who are aware, the less likely the implementation of a world government will succeed.

The strings are being laid across the American giant. We cannot wait until they succeed in tying down our nation. By that time, it will be too late.

The time to get involved is now.

Index

Index

Constitutional Convention, US, 122
Declaration of Independence, 30, 83, 110
De Gucht, Karel, 7
Disinformation, 135n
Dole, Sen. Bob, 127
Dow-Jones, 24
Dow Chemical Company, 18
Dulles, John Foster, 122, 125

Earth Summit, 99
Eisenhower, administration,122
Engels, Frederick, 31-33, 48, 106-107, 134
England, 44, 51, 53, 59-60
Environment, 50, 99, 116, 134
Executive Order 12852, 100
Euro, 109
Europäische Wirtschaftsgemeinschaft, 45
European Coal And Steel Community, 55
European Commission, 7, 42n, 52
European Community, 42n, 45
European Constitution, 51-54
European Economic Commission, 42n
European Economic Community, 45
European Parliament, 7, 43, 53
European Soviet, 51

FBI, 90
FEMA, 86
Field, Justice Stephen J., 124
First Life of Angela M., The 50
Foreign Affairs, 6, 97
Fox, Mex. President Vicente, 62
France, 44, 53, 59
Free Trade Area of the Americas (FTAA), 61, 108
Frey, Mark, 48
FSB, 90

Ft. Carson, 87
General Assembly, 76, 115, 125, 133
Gingrich, Newt, 13
Gore, Albert, 127
Great Deception: The Secret History of the European Union, The, 52
Gulliver's Travels, 131

Haass, Richard N., 64
Hagel, Charles, 80
Hamilton, Alexander, 123-124
Hate, 137
Hiss, Alger, 13, 97
Hitler, 44-45, 57

Holy Family, The, 106
Iceland, 86n
ICLEI - International Council for Local Environmental Initiatives, 78 (See also *Agenda 21*)
International Center for the Settlement of Investment Disputes, 9
International Court of Justice, 55, 116
International courts, 8-11, 116
International Covenant on Civil and Political Rights, 111, 115, 125, 127
International Criminal Court, 116
International Fund for Agriculture Development, 116
International Labor Organization, 116
International Maritime Organization, 116
International Monetary Fund (IMF), 109, 110, 115
International Seabed

141

Index

Index

Index

About The John Birch Society

Since 1958, members of The John Birch Society have led the drive to restore constitutional limitations on government, preserve our nation's independence, and uphold the principles that have made our country the envy of mankind.

The John Birch Society is a nationwide information and action organization, consisting of thousands of ordinary Americans — Americans who have a deep, personal commitment to preserving freedom for future generations. Members inform themselves and others, and then work together to preserve freedom and bring about change in national policy where it is needed. For more information please visit www.jbs.org.

STOP the Free Trade Agenda

Join with thousands of other Americans working to stop the free trade agenda. Inform yourself, then take action by going to the "Choose Freedom — STOP the Free Trade Agenda" action project page at JBS.org (www.jbs.org/issues-pages/stop-the-free-trade-agenda). Every individual can make a difference in the battle to preserve freedom.